Sudha Murty

A Critical Study of Her Celebrated Works

Author: Dr. Smeetaa Wanjarri

ISBN No:978-81-7192-233-8

Preface

Sudha Murty occupies an important place in Indian writing in English these days and has left an indelible mark in the field of children's literature. A writer, philanthropist and entrepreneur, Sudha Murty is greatly revered for being a prolific writer, facilitating the education of poor children and for being one of the brains behind Infosys, one of India's leading IT company. Sudha Murty's philanthropic work has garnered global recognition. From becoming the first female Engineer of India to heading a conglomerate like Infosys, her seriousness towards making a change in society and her educational journey has played a significant role in shaping her outlook.

Sudha Murty was born on August 19, 1950 in a Brahmin family in Shiggaon, Karnataka. Her father Dr R.H. Kulkarni who was a surgeon and her mother Vimala Kulkarni supported her in her endeavours right from her childhood and raised well young Sudha along with her three siblings. An educated atmosphere in the family instilled in her a passion to do something extraordinary at an early age. Her early life experiences and affinity to her grandmother became the foundation for some of her books.

Her writings have contributed immensely to enrichment of contemporary English literature. Through her writings she tackles education, religious tasks, cultural aspects, family relationship, social mores and attitudes, economical situation, and feminist problems, etc. A multi-faceted person, Sudha Murty's writing is a mirror of society where the picture of the Indian women in all walks of life - political, social, educational, architectural, administrative, and domestic is clearly depicted and the prolific writer deals with all aspects of society. The great social worker, author, technician and educationalist, Sudha Murty contributed to the Indian English literature through fictional, non-fictional novels, short stories, novellas and travelogues through the verities of literary genre.

She stands up for women and their issues and is quite vociferous in her support of them, fighting against any discrimination. She is full of humility and modesty and uses her wealth for the less fortunate people. She acknowledges the cry and requirement of the impoverished, the destitute and the marginalized sections of the society. She writes in the backdrop of Indian English Literature. The main protagonists are portrayed as well educated women with the inherent inner power who are ready to face the challenges under any circumstances and emerge successfully by carving a place for themselves in the society within the parameter of the Indian tradition. These female protagonists, in her writings, are often found to be suffering from different social and domestic problems.

As is suggested by the name, this book contains succinct critical analysis of major works of Sudha Murty. The analysis is based on the standards of literary criticism.

Hopefully this will serve the purpose of one and all concerned.

Obviously, books of such nature cannot be written without consulting relevant literature. Admittedly the basic information for this work is churned out of a number of primary and secondary sources, e.g., books, articles, research papers etc., available in print and digital form both. I am deeply beholden to all the scholars whose writings, research findings and opinions are cited or substantially made use of. In fact, the real credit for this goes to them all.

I express my deep sense of gratitude to my mother-in-law Dr. Suhasini Wanjari for her guidance and I am also grateful to my husband Mr. Abhijit Wanjarri (MLC) for his support and all possible assistance in completion of this work. My children - Miss Devika and Master Rajvardhan - they are my life force and I am equally thankful to them for their patience and support.

I am equally grateful to my parents Mr. H.M. Kamdi and Mrs. Rekha Kamdi and my other family members and near & dear ones!

Last but not the least, I am thankful to Mr. Ankit Nangia and his team at Dattsons Publishers, Nagpur for evincing keen interest in this and publishing the book meticulously in the present shape, and that too within shortest possible time.

--Author

Table of Contents

1

Introduction: Fictional World of Sudha Murty

An educator, author and philanthropist, and chairperson of Infosys Foundation, Sudha Murty is married to the co-founder of Infosys, N. R. Narayana Murthy. Murty was awarded the Padma Shri, the fourth highest civilian award in India, for social work by the Government of India in 2006.

Sudha Murty began her professional career in computer science and engineering. She is the chairperson of Infosys Foundation and a member of the public health care initiatives of the Gates Foundation. She has founded several orphanages, participated in rural development efforts, supported the movement to provide all Karnataka government schools with computer and library facilities, and established Murty Classical Library of India at Harvard University.

Murty is best known for her social work and her contribution to literature in Kannada and English. *Dollar Bahu,* a novel originally authored by her in Kannada and later translated into English as *Dollar Bahu,* was adapted as a televised dramatic series by Zee TV in 2001. *Runa,* a story was adapted as a Marathi movie - *Pitruroon* by director Nitish Bhardwaj. Sudha Murty has also acted in the film as well as a Kannada film *Prarthana.*

Sudha Murty was born into a Kannada Deshastha Madhva Brahmin family on August 19, 1950, in Shiggaon, Haveri in Karnataka, to surgeon R. H. Kulkarni and his wife Vimala Kulkarni. She was raised by her parents and maternal grandparents. Her childhood experiences form the historical basis for her first notable work entitled How I Taught My Grandmother to Read, Wise and Otherwise and Other Stories. Murty completed a B.E. in Electrical and Electronics Engineering from the B.V.B. College of Engineering & Technology (now known as KLE Technological University), and then M.E. in Computer Science from the Indian Institute of Science.

Her education has a major role to play in shaping her as a successful author, even though her educational path was more technical in nature. Her hard work and commitment are clear from the fact that she emerged as a topper during her bachelor's and master's degrees.

Career

Sudha Murty became the first female engineer hired at India's largest auto manufacturer TATA Engineering and Locomotive Company (TELCO). She joined the company as a Development Engineer in Pune and then worked in Mumbai and Jamshedpur as well.

Sudha Murthy has always been an advocate of women's rights and a pioneer in the development of education. Once she wrote to Tata Motors, also known as Telco about their men-only policy, and for that she was called to an interview, and later became the first female engineer to be employed in India. Her position at Telco was important in redefining the company's jobs policies. She later joined Walchand Group of Industries at Pune as Senior Systems Analyst.

Besides supporting her husband Narayana Murthy in establishing Infosys and giving him the initial investment, she has written a humongous volume of literature which includes books for kids as well. Through her books, she has encouraged the young and elderly to inculcate a habit of reading in them. Sudha Murthy's education and relentless efforts at contributing towards the improvement in society has made her a brand name. Through her Infosys Foundation, she has helped in spreading awareness about education, public hygiene, poverty alleviation, etc.

An active member of the Gates Foundation, her efforts at revolutionizing the Education System of India have been phenomenal in the country where she supported the use of Computer Technology in educational institutions in Karnataka. She also established the Murty Classical Library of India (MCLI) at Harvard.

Achievements

It is worth-mentioning here that Sudha Murthy's education and her work in various domains have led her to win many awards and accolades. She has received many awards for her academic excellence. In the year 2019, IIT Kanpur awarded her *Honorary Doctor of Science* (DSc) degree. Her achievements include a list of literary works in many languages. Initially, she started to write in Kannada and later wrote in English as well. Her works are all about family, marriage, social problems, etc. She has received several awards and distinctions for her achievements, including the R.K. Narayan Award for literature.

Sudha Murty is also the chairperson and trustee of Infosys Foundation. With her master's in electrical engineering from the Indian Institute of Science, Bangalore, she started Infosys Foundation in 1996. She has built 2300 houses in flood-affected areas through the foundation. She has built 7000 libraries in schools, and also 16,000 toilets.

She is Visiting Professor at the PG Center of Bangalore University. She also taught at Christ University.

Sudha Murty has written and published many books which include novels, non-fiction, travelogues, technical books, and memoirs. Her books have been translated into all major Indian languages. She is also a columnist for English and Kannada newspapers.

Sudha Murty married N. R. Narayana Murthy when she was employed as an engineer at TELCO in Pune. The couple have two children.

Awards

- **2004:** Raja-Lakshmi Award by Sri Raja-Lakshmi Foundation in Chennai
- **2006**: India's fourth highest civilian award Padma Shri
- **2006**: She also received the R.K. Narayana's Award for Literature.
- **2010**: Daana Chintamani Attimabbe Award by Karnataka Government.

- **2011**: Murty was conferred honorary LL.D. (Doctor of Laws) degrees for contributions to promote formal legal education and scholarship in India.
- **2013**: Basava Shree-2013 Award was presented to Narayan Murthy & Sudha Murty for their contributions to society.
- **2018**: Murty received the Crossword Book award in popular (Non-Fiction) category.
- **2019**: IIT Kanpur awarded her Honorary Degree (*Honoris Causa*) of Doctor of Science.
- National Award from Public Relation Society of India for outstanding Social Service to the Society.
- Award for Excellent Social Service by Rotary South – Hubli.
- "Millenium Mahila Shiromani" award.

Notably some of Sudha Murty's widely acclaimed books include *The Mother I Never Knew, Three Thousand Stitches, The Man from the Egg* and *Magic of the Lost Temple*. With this compilation, here is a collection of 15 of the best Sudha Murty Books out of the many she has written.

Major Literary Output

In Kannada

- Kaveri inda Mekaangige

- Tumla

- Runa

- Yashasvi

- Nooniya Sahasagalu

- Dollar Sose

- Guttondu Heluve

- Athirikthe

- Hakkiya Teradalli

- Paridhi

- Yerilitada Daariyalli

- Computer lokadalli

- Sukhesini   Mattu   Itara   Makkala Kathegalu

- Samanyralli Asamanyaru

- Astitva

- Mahashweta

English Books

- The Mother I Never Knew
- Magic of the Lost Temple
- The Day I Stopped Drinking Milk
- The Upside-Down King
- The Man from the Egg
- The Magic Drum and other favorite stories
- Wise and Otherwise
- Something Happened on the Way To Heaven
- Gently Falls The Bakula
- House of Cards
- The Old Man and His God
- How The Sea Became Salty
- The Magic of the Lost Temple
- The Bird with the Golden Wings
- How I Taught My Grandmother to Read and Other Stories
- Grandparents Bag of Stories
- Dollar Bahu
- Three Thousand Stitches
- The Daughter from a Wishing Tree
- The Serpent's Revenge
- Grandma's Bag of Stories

A significant feature, the education of Sudha Murty and her ideology to lead society towards a better future has inspired many to take philanthropy as a way of living. Personalities like her inspire us to believe in dreams and working hard towards achieving them. If you have a dream of studying abroad, Leverage Edu can help you realize it. From applying at a university to getting a visa done, our experts will help you with all of it.

Now let us have a look at her views about herself.

Interestingly the times where one found dolphins in the Ganges and deer on busy roads are long gone. Humans have been greedy in their pursuits and have infiltrated the natural habitat of other living beings. Her new book has many layers, which would even make adults pause and think about the natural world. She recollected her childhood memories of full moons in the context of the little episode of her new book where Devi gives her three sisters a special task to complete between two full-moon nights, as a significant symbol of happiness. She reminisced how on a cold, quiet and cosy night the insects sang to each other or with a gentle wind the leaves rustled conveying their messages to the wind.

As a child living with grandparents she was exposed to plenty of literary pilgrimages. Her grandfather took her to libraries and taught her to be gentle and careful with books.

She firmly believes that the lives of children were easy as they had their grandparents around who taught them valuable life lessons. Her writings for children aim to do that. As a grandparent, she herself found inspiration to write for children because it lets her think like one. For her, children are curious, unbiased, open-minded and adventurous and she wants to instill important knowledge in them through her books by making them light and enjoyable.

In the most interactive segment, the children eagerly asked questions to their beloved author. On being asked about how since earlier generations the rate of acceptability towards failure has been decreasing, she denounced pressurizing children and mentioned, "Academic excellence is not the only excellence in life." For her, the need for parents to define a child through his achievements is the greatest pressure which is why the generation is more scared of failures.

Sudha acknowledged how the new world technology is attractive, a joy for the eyes and the ill effects of it on mental as well as physical health. She said, "Reading makes our imagination fertile. It's a joy to the mind."

Here it will be appropriate to have a glimpse at her fictional world.

The Fictional World of Sudha Murty

In common parlance by 'fictional world' we mean a self-consistent setting with events, and often other elements, that differ from the real world. It may also be called an imagined, constructed, or fictional realm (or world). Fictional universes may appear in novels, comics, films, television shows, video games, and other creative works.

In fact, the subject is most commonly addressed in reference to fictional universes that differ markedly from the real world, such as those that introduce entire fictional cities, countries, or even planets, or those that contradict commonly known facts about the world and its history, or those that feature fantasy or science fiction concepts such as magic or faster than light travel--and especially those in which a deliberate development of the setting is a substantial focus of the work. But fictional world may have many similarities with real world. Thus, magic, miracles, myth and fantasy are uniquely blended in fictional world.

Let us peep through the fictional world of Sudha Murty.

A prolific writer, Sudha Murty has written a number of story books, meant for children and youngsters. She has a way with words and writes in such a smooth and captivating style that not only the children but even grown-ups enjoy reading her stories. She has a simple and unique style where she blends morality with fun in such a way that the children get the message along with enjoyment without being conscious of it. In her stories morality, without being a painstaking effort on the part of the writer and an irksome burden for the young reader, gets expressed as "her philosophic views on charity, hospitality and self-realization through fictional narratives." So, the moral vibes in her fictional world are too conspicuous to be overlooked easily.

Obviously Sudha Murty is a writer with a purpose. While reading a story by her, the reader becomes a part of the gang of youngsters including Raghu, Meenu, Anand and Krishna who surround their *Ajji* and often get lost in the fictional world of grandmother's stories. As has been stated earlier, morality and fun go hand-in-hand in Sudha Murty's stories. For example, in the story *Doctor, Doctor* we have a shopkeeper called Ravi in a small village somewhere near a great desert in India. On a very hot day Ravi receives a visitor in the form of a very old man in his shop. The old man is so tired and thirsty that he cannot speak. He somehow opens his mouth to utter the word 'water'.

It being an acute drought, the villagers bring water from a faraway stream, making it extremely precious- every drop of it. Ravi offers water to the old man who, very surprisingly, empties the whole pitcher. Ravi is dismayed to lose all water but feels a sense of satisfaction also thinking that he had helped someone in real need. His kindness to the old, thirsty man turns the ordinary pot into a magical pot. Whosoever drinks water from this pot is cured of his/her ailments and deformities. And it never gets empty. The shopkeeper and his pot become very famous even in faraway places. Then Ravi turns greedy and starts favouring rich patients to earn a few bucks. One day again the old man returns but instead of quenching his thirst, Ravi goes to the palace to take care of the queen who was exasperated due to a mosquito bite. If Ravi's kindness had given the pot magical powers, his greed turns it into an ordinary pot again. It is to be noted that the readers as well as the character get their message in no equivocal terms.

Sudha Murty fortifies her teachings with a well-advised dose of healthy fun. *Five Spoons of Salt* is a story which has the reader in splits while giving a beautiful message to him. This story is about a young girl named Gita who has this embarrassing habit of forgetting things. She leaves the home to bring medicine for her grandfather who has a severe headache but returns home empty-handed after visiting a sweet shop and chatting with a friend for a long time whom she accidently comes across in the market. She forgets to remove the clothes from the washing line. Instead of taking her sister's lunchbox to school she spends the whole day forgetfully in a circus watching the animals.

And, only the smoke billowing out of her room's window reminds her that she had forgotten a shirt under a hot iron. Finally comes the day, when she does not forget to put five spoons of salt in the *sambar*, but then her grandfather, grandmother, her father, brother, and her sister add five spoons of salt each to the sambar thinking that Gita would certainly forget her mother's instruction about the five spoons of salt.

Initially the story is related in a very delightful way so much so that the reader finds it a pure fun to read it. Besides the fun, Gita learns the lesson of her life and starts behaving like a careful and responsible girl. Almost every story by Sudha Murty has a separate beginning and ending part which may not directly be related to the story but tells a lot to the reader about the South Indian culture and way of life. This story tells us about *Santhe,* a village market day which is observed once a week. It makes an interesting reading how the seven children undertake an on foot journey to Santhe in the company of Damu, who is Vishnu *kaka's* right-hand man. Damu tells them the story on their way to the market.

Again, we have Indian culture and morality at display when at the end of the story a fruit vendor refuses to accept money from Ajja because he was an old student of Ajja and his conscience does not allow him to take money from his teacher.

For instance, in her book, *How I Taught My Grandmother to Read and Other Stories* Sudha Murty tells her stories in a colloquial way and strike a rapport with the reader straightaway. Her style of telling stories-within-story definitely marks the beginning of a new and charming way of storytelling in the history of children's literature.

The story *A Journey through Desert* begins with the reminiscent author telling a tale from her own past. She recounts how she met two identical twins in a workshop where she used to get her car serviced from. Ram and Gopal, the fatherless boys, work as errand boys in the workshop and they can't afford the school education as they belong to a very poor family. In spite of all the difficulty they face, they keep smiling. The author starts visiting them on regular intervals and she tells them quite a few stories. With the passage of time she hires a driver and stops going to the workshop, thus forgetting the boys completely. After a decade or so one day her driver tells her about a garage owner who was inquiring about her.

Out of curiosity, she pays a visit to the garage and to her pleasant surprise finds one of the twins as owner. Ram, the owner, tells her that one of her stories had changed his life. The story was about two boys who decided to cross a big desert to go to the next town where according to the elders the life was better and the future more promising. The elders advised them to pick up stones from the desert and carry to that town. Some buyers would pay money for those rare stones. The boys carried food and water and did not feel tired in the beginning. The sun rose over their heads and the sand under their feet became hot. After walking for a few hours they thought that they had reached the edge of the desert and finished their food and water. After some time they realized they had covered only half the way.

They picked up stones and their bags became very heavy. One of the boys lost his heart and decided to go back. The other continued to walk towards his destination. It was a difficult journey and he had his doubts. But faith and hope kept him going and ultimately he reached the town. He was disappointed to find that this was just another town and there was nothing special about it. He yearned to return but it was already dark and he decided to spend the night in the town. In the morning he opened his bag to throw away the stones. He couldn't believe his eyes when he found that the stones had turned into diamonds. The brothers had enjoyed the story but Ram had got his message too. He says to the narrator:

"Do you remember Madam, you also told us the meaning of the story? A student's life is like the desert, examinations are the hot sun, difficulties are like the warm sand and study is like hunger and thirst. As a student you have to travel all alone collecting knowledge and skill the way the boy in the story collected stones. The more you collect the better is the life you lead later." (How I Taught... 76)

There is another story in this story which explains the mental state of Gopal, the other boy. He is compared to a jackal in the desert that on looking at his large shadow in the early morning sun decided that he would hunt a camel for his afternoon meal. He kept searching for a camel without paying any attention to the smaller animals that he could easily catch. At noon, he looked at his shadow again and found that his shadow had become even smaller than his actual size. He dropped the camel idea and started looking for a mouse.

Though these stories by Sudha Murty are meant for children, yet these stories are no less entertaining and educative for any grown-up. One is transported to one's childhood where there are green, grassy fields, ponds, canals, village streets, marriages, festivals, rituals, uncles, aunts, grandparents and a group of lovable youngsters, who have arrived in the calmness and serenity of a sleepy village somewhere in South India from the hustle and bustle of a metropolitan city. These are refreshing stories about ordinary people told in an extraordinarily simple and impressive style. These stories, besides being interesting and entertaining, have astonishing lessons to reveal. We have examples of both incredible generosity and unbelievable meanness which define general human nature on this planet. They showcase the myriad shades of human nature.

Themes in Perspective

In common parlance, by the word 'theme' we mean a core notion around which the novel's action is woven. It is the subject of a book. A novelist writes for a reason. He or she intends to offer some message, attack some undesirable behaviours in person or society, spread some ethics among the readers, present a social problem, narrate historically significant events with a new perspective etc. A novelist, in short, writes with certain intentions. "He communicates not in vacuum. In every novel there is usually one dominant theme and several less dominant ones to support it. The supporting themes can emerge to illustrate the basic theme by parallel themes or conflicting themes. Indian fiction writers in English have written on the topics of caste, class, social inequality, oppression, isolation, discrimination, unemployment, rural and urban gap etc. A novelist can simultaneously discuss one or more of the above subjects. In reality the grandeur of a novel depends on the efficient handling of different themes in a single work."

To be a writer, one must have a motive for writing. In order to convey a message, criticise bad conduct, disseminate morals, or tell a story from a different angle, the author plans to do all of these things. In a nutshell, an author sets out to accomplish a certain goal. In other words, he doesn't talk to himself. Thematically, every work has a primary topic and a supporting cast of subplots that revolve around it. Parallel or opposing ideas may develop from the supporting themes to emphasise the main subject. In actuality, a novel's grandeur is determined by its ability to handle a wide range of topics in a single work.

She doesn't only write about women's concerns; Sudha Murty covers a wide range of topics in her writings. Her work shows a major shift in the general perspective of female writing. Feminine literature sometimes blames men for women's problems, as if men and women were born competitors and marriage was a licence to carry out a man's agenda of subjugating women. And one lady and her husband are to blame for another woman's woes, according to Sudha Murty. In all four of her works, the delicate connection between two women in a family is shown.

To put it another way, Sudha Murty also examines the influence of increasing capitalism on Indian society's deep personal interactions. Indians now have hundreds of ways to gain wealth because of economic liberalisation in the country. Young men and women were given the opportunity to go to first-world nations and take use of contemporary amenities. On the one hand, it changed their social and financial status.

In contrast, it caused tensions in the family's close-knit community.

All works of Sudha Murty deal with the deterioration of family relationships. Her paintings include a variety of subplots. In general, Indians have a strong sense of superstition. They adhere to a strict caste structure that emphasises the importance of arranged weddings. There is a significant role played in Indian daily life by horoscopes, favourable dark periods, rituals, habits, conventions, and religious beliefs. In all of her writings, Sudha Murty brilliantly exposes the absurdities of Indian society.

In essence, her literary output includes many minor themes. The Indians are superstitious, in general. They believe in the caste system, particularly in the fixation of marriages. Horoscopes, propitious dark times, rituals, practices, conventions, religious beliefs are playing their part in everyday lives of Indians. Sudha Murty immaculately brings out inconsistencies in the lives of Indians in all her works.

On Her Narrative Technique/Structure

Narratives are works that provide an account of connected events. To put it simply, a narrative is a story. There are many types of literature that are considered narratives, including novels, dramas, fables, folk tales, short stories, and poetry. In addition to literature, narratives are found in cinema, music, and theatre.

Narrative techniques provide deeper meaning for the reader and help the reader use imagination to visualize situations. Narrative literary techniques are also known as literary devices. Before we look too closely at narrative techniques, it's important to understand that literary elements in narratives include such things as the setting, plot, theme, style or structure, characters, and perspective, or voice of the story, since literary techniques are best understood in the context of one of these elements.

Narrative structure is about story and plot: the content of a story and the form used to tell the story. Story refers to the dramatic action as it might be described in chronological order. Plot refers to how the story is told. Story is about trying to determine the key conflicts, main characters, setting and events. Plot is about how, and at what stages, the key conflicts are set up and resolved.

Most forms of narrative fall under four main categories: linear narrative, nonlinear narrative, interactive narration, and interactive narrative.

Linear narrative is the most common form of narration, where events are largely portrayed in a chronological order telling the events in the order in which they occurred. Nonlinear narrative, disjointed narrative, or disrupted narrative is a narrative technique where events are portrayed out of chronological order or in other ways where the narrative does not follow the direct causality pattern. And interactive narration refers to a work where the linear narrative is driven by, rather than influenced by, the user's interaction.

While interactive narrative is a form of fiction in which users are able to make choices that influence the narrative (for example, through alternative plots or resulting in alternative endings) through their actions.

Keep this in mind that there are many literary techniques, here we will examine literary techniques relevant to style, plot, and narrative perspective, or point of view. Common techniques relevant to style, or the language chosen to tell a story, include metaphors, similes, personification, imagery, hyperbole, and alliteration. Common techniques relevant to plot, which is the sequence of events that make a narrative, include backstory, flashback, flash-forward, and foreshadowing. Common techniques relevant to narrative perspective, or who is telling the story, include first person, second person, third person, and third-person omniscient.

It is significant to note that the way the story and the events are depicted is called the technique of narration. A writer by use of 'first person narration' tells his story. In this, the character narrates the events and incidents of his life himself. "First person storytelling typically uses the method of recollection to recall one's past. Sometimes writer creates a narrator who unfolds the action through its eye. The writer makes use of this strategy to keep his distance from the characters. The third form of narrative strategy is the author himself takes the reins of the work's action into his hands. Most authors adopt this technique." In the 20th century, a technique called 'Streams Of Consciousness' evolved.

M. H. Abrams describes Stream of Consciousness as "Stream of Consciousness is the name for a special mode of narration that undertakes to reproduce, without a narrator's intervention the full spectrum and the continuous flow of a character's mental process, in which sense perceptions mingle with conscious and half-conscious thoughts, memories, expectations, feelings and random associations." One of the remarkable highlights of good composing is its capability to compel readers to stick to the story. In fact, it is not the author alone who composes. "The readers who are the audience are equivalent stakeholders in the arrangement of the content. Allegorical passing of a creator implies the introduction of readers in the imaginative demonstration. Genuine creator makes co-creators who guide and screen his or her composing.

This procedure of aggregate composing is incredibly important in the energy about a narrator."(Negi, 2017)

Lamentably Sudha Murty neglects to make co-writers and co-readers. She presents, clarifies and deciphers her characters leaving almost no place for readers to do anything. This may suit customary Indian technique for narrating. Although it makes her works one-sided, she stays a focal point of fascination for the new readers of India. "Sudha Murthy sets her books by weaving the strings of customs and advancement in all her works. Indians, even today, revere their social legacy. Numerous Indians are pleased with it. Sudha Murty sets the activity of her books in the towns what's more, provincial inclinations that exist in huge urban communities. Juxtaposition of country existence with cosmopolitan life of the urban areas makes her work illustrative of in general Indian life. It likewise causes her to draw out the showdown between two ages."

According to Sudha Murty, "For imagination, the sky is the limit; but the reality is far more unimaginable and that is why I like writing non-fiction. From fiction, you do not get to learn much because it is only imagination. Whereas, from non-fiction, people can understand and learn from the realities it covers."

"In spite of the fact that she is a Maharastrian by birth, her business realm and humanitarian work is essentially in Karnataka. Normally she is very much familiar with the individuals and their ways of life around there. Her characters have Kannada names like Akka, Appa, Avva and so forth. This doesn't be that as it may imply that her books are territorial in extension and bid. We discover individuals with such qualities somewhere else in India. Her expertise to grow the canvas of her books is essential."(Govind, 2019)

Now we turn to characterization technique of Sudha Murty.

Her Characterisation Technique

It is apt to mention here that character in a work of art is usually a being with human or divine attributes. It is an individual's ablity to perform actions. It is built through the interaction between the character readers and the textual representation. It is defined by Margolin as "Character refers to any person, individual or group, normally human or supernatural, inserted in a narrative fiction work. As such, characters reside within the worlds of fiction and play a part in one or more of the states of affairs or incidents spoken about in the plot, no matter how small. Character can be described succinctly as a participant in the world of stories."

In essence, characterization is a process where a writer shapes an individual into a personality, a simple name into an identity. The capacity of the writer to make this transition defines a writer's skill, or otherwise. "Writer uses different forms, such as descriptions, discussions, dialogues, interior monologues to give it a touch of verisimilitude."

Characters were generally classified into heroes, villains and minor characters as per their appearances throughout the novel, traditionally. They were often called major and minor characters depending on the role they were performing in the novel.

In recent times, conventional division of characters into flat and round characters is finished. Including words such as protagonist and main hero, characters indicate a change in our hero paradigm, which was supposed to be noble, courageous and complex in the past. "Today we have characters from subaltern section of the society. Bakha in *Untouchable*, Munoo in *Coolie*, Balaram in *The White Tiger*, Rukhamani in *Nectar in a Sieve*, and the likes have occupied central stage in the novels today."

Amazingly with recent developments in the field of psychology and anthropology, characterisation art has gained new aspects. The character's minds contain descriptions of disruptions along with the descriptions of their physical appearances. "Readers are supposed to read their minds to discern the truth behind the actions of characters. Characterization is rich and realistic through the efforts of the writer to place his characters with new characters in various circumstances. Characterization depends on the abilities of the writer with which he creates his characters in relation to one another."

Note that one of Sudha Murty's character's striking features is that they come from middle-class backgrounds. They are from either the world of education or the service sector. Sudha Murty binds them simultaneously with the conventional Indian society and with today's ultramodern society. "The majority of young characters are engaged in their growth professionally and personally. The old characters are drawn to wealth but in other ways are unable to improve themselves. . . ."

The comparison of female characters of Sudha Murty with the female characters of other Indian female novelists, one finds that the women of Murty have a positive approach to life. They value hard work. Their take on life is highly enthusiastic. "*Rukhamini's* Kamala Markandaya resigns to fate. She is a destitute being in the grip of cruel fate. Tanner evacuates her from her old home. Her kids are ditching her. Society is treating her poorly. She faces all of that passively, without grumbling. Strong powers rule her outside. Sudha

Murty's women plan their own fate. Mahashweta and Mridula do not go down to circumstances. The situations are not down to Mahashweta and Mridula.They rather work to bring about a change in external situation."(Govind, 2019)

"The characterisation of Sudha Murty lacks imagination. She struggles to dive deep into her character's psychological crises. Young boys and girls get married and start a relationship. The two do not have intimate outings. This is very odd. Without wandering and dating it is impossible to expect modern boys and girls with high academic credentials and knowledge to get into marital relations."(S. Parvathi, 2016) Despite these shortcomings, her characterization art is clear and direct in keeping with the storytelling tradition in India. As a result, novels of Sudha Murty and short stories cater to today's Indian reader's section only. She stands out as an excellent narrator because of her devotion to Indian culture and not because of copying the westerners. This goes on to prove that India has evolved but that the Indians have not. (Govind, 2019)

As is generally perceived, human or heavenly characters are the most common kind of characters in works of art. It is a person who is capable of taking action. As the characters and the textual representation converse, the world is formed. Margolin defines it this way: 'A character might be anybody or anything in a narrative fiction work— human or other worldly, average or extraordinary.' As a result, characters exist in the fictional worlds they inhabit and have a hand in at least one of the situations or events described in the storyline. 'A character may be regarded as a participant in the fictional universe.'

When a writer creates an individual, he or she creates an individuality, a persona. A writer's ability to make this shift is a measure of their expertise, or lack thereof. For realism, the author employs a variety of literary devices such as descriptions, talks, conversations, and internal monologues.

According to their appearances in the literature, characters were usually categorised as heroes, villains, or minor characters based on their roles. Depending on their importance in the story, they were referred to as 'major characters' or 'minor characters.' Traditionally, characters were divided into flat and round characters. However, this classification has been abolished recently. With terminology like protagonist and primary hero, characters reveal a shift in our hero paradigm that was intended to be noble, heroic and complicated in the past. Subalterns make up the bulk of the cast nowadays.

Disruptions are described in the characters brains as well as their bodily looks. 'Readers are intended to be able to decipher the motivations of the characters in order to understand their actions.' 'Through the author's attempts to situate his characters in diverse situations, he creates a rich and realistic depiction of his characters.' The ability of the writer to develop characters in connection to one another is critical to characterization.'

Characters in Sudha Murty's work are notable for their middle class origins. They either come from the educational or service industries. Sudha Murty connects them to both the traditional Indian civilization and today's ultramodern society. For the most part, the young people in the show are focused on their personal and professional development. Riches beckon the venerable characters, yet they are unable to better themselves because of their inherent limitations.

Modern technology creates tensions between the old and the new, as well as between traditional ways of doing things and newer ones.

Having studied the biographical elements, writing style, themes, narrative techniques and charcterisationof Sudha Murty in this chapter, we will take her major works-- fiction and stories in the subsequent chapters of the book.

References

"Author Murty makes acting debut with Pitruroon - Indian Express", archive.indianexpress.com.   Retrieved 15 April 2022.

"Murty, wife gift Harvard $5.2 mn to publish Indian classics - Indian Express". archive.indianexpress.com. Retrieved 8 March 2022.

"Murty Classical Library of India".

www.murtylibrary.com. Retrieved 2 May 2022.

"Murty family gift establishes Murty Classical Library of India series", *Harvard Gazette,* 29 April 2010. Retrieved 8 March 2022.

"Presenting Harmony's silvers – sparkling lives, success stories, accounts of endurance, courage, grit, and passion", harmonyindia.org. Archived from the original on 24 September 2015. Retrieved 2 December 2015.

"The Hindu : Gates Foundation's AIDS initiative launched", 31 December 2003. Archived from the original on 31 December 2003. Retrieved 2 May 2022.

Govind, R. (2019, 11 27). Sudha Murthy's new book profiles strong, brave women from mythology. Retrieved from https://www.thehindu.com/books/books-authors/sudhamurthy/article30096474.ece

Krishnana, V. (2015, 08 19). This Story Of Infosys Founder Narayan Murthy's Wife 'Sudha Murty' Will Make You Salute Her.

Retrieved from https://www.comedyflavors.com/infosys-founder-narayanmurthys-wife-sudha-murthy/

Negi, D. (2017, 08 19), Brilliant, Brave & Badass, Sudha Murty is The Kind Of Role Model We Women Need Today.

Retrieved from https://www.scoopwhoop.com/sudha-murthyand-her-inspiring-journey/

Nivetha, D. (2008). Sudhā Mūrti - 2008 - Gently falls the bakula.pdf.

Retrieved from https://www.worldwidejournals.com/paripex/recent_issues_pdf/2018/March/March_2018_1520433975__112.pdf

Parvathi, S. (2016), Quest for Self in the Select Novels of Sudha Murty, International Journal of English Language, Literature.

Prerna, R. (23 January 2011), Sudha Murthy: Humility personified, *Business Standard India,* Retrieved 2 May 2022.

Rana, S Gautam (24 October 2022). Sudha Murthy still fond of Tatas | Patna News - Times of India, *The Times of India*, Retrieved 8 March 2022.

2

Wise and Otherwise: A Salute to Life

"Experience has taught me that honesty is not the mark of any particular class nor is it related to education or wealth. It cannot be taught at any university. In most people, it springs naturally from the heart."- Sudha Murty

Wise & Otherwise: A Salute to Life is a non-fiction book written by popular writer Sudha Murty. It was published by East West Books Pvt. Ltd (Madras) in the year 2002 and a revised edition is first published by Penguin Books with an addition of an extra chapter in the year 2006. *Wise and Otherwise: A Salute to Life* is a collection of fifty-one short stories based on the real life experiences of the author. As Chairperson of the Infosys Foundation, she has come across many types of people in her office as well as while travelling during the course of her work. Each story covers a facet of human nature and has something to tell. Her dedication states

"For the 'shirtless people of India' who have taught me so much about my country"

Initially the book shows encounters Sudha Murty has had with ordinary people and extraordinary minds during her travels and personal experiences.

Focus on Plot

Fifty one vignettes showcase the myriad shades of human nature. Contents in the book include stories ranging from a man who dumps his aged father in an old-age home after declaring him to be a homeless stranger; a tribal chief in the Sahyadri hills who teaches the author that there is humility in receiving too and how a sick woman remembers to thank her benefactor even from her deathbed.

Basically the book features vivid life instances of Sudha Murty herself. In these 51 tales, she jots down 51 incidences she came across which somehow affected her deeply. May it be a small comment she heard or some person's Aura she felt. In these 51 tales, a reader learns about Human Behaviour. It may or may not be bold but the way she wrote them in this book, makes you focus on those particular moments and instances. Her writing is what makes those not so important moments, some great lessons and life stories for a reader. I enjoyed reading this book, though I felt these Short stories as too short. That's the reason I took so long to finish this.

Significantly Sudha Murty's stories cover the length and breadth of India and she has stories about various types of characters like the honest college student, who despite being poor returned the unspent money that he received for his hostel accommodation. There is a story about a man who lies while trying to impress her and another one about an old man in the Sahyadri forest who tells her, "There is a grace in accepting also". The story about the young nurse who followed her teacher's words and about an old man in Kalahandi district of Orissa who does not know that India is now a free country but says, "This little paper (Indian currency) can turn our lives upside down". She mentions about two teenagers she had met on the flight from Delhi to Bangalore who did not know our history (we should blame ourselves for it), about her friend who takes life in a positive way after she sees a beggar dancing in the rain and there is this story about a man who lies that he knows her in order to sell books to the Foundation.

In one story, she mentions about a salesgirl she meets in a train, who first gives her a headache and then sells her the balm. In another, she talks about a mother who is praying that her stove burst victim daughter dies. She talks about her friend who succeeds in life because she is a realist. About a poor, old lady who shows her gratitude to Mrs Murty for giving them a hospital by giving a string of jasmine flowers. There is story in which she talks about a man who leaves his own father in an old age home claiming that the he is a homeless man who needs help and comes to claim the money when he dies.

She brought tears to my eyes when she talked about Zubeida, who tells her brother to return the unspent money allotted for her cancer treatment. She has written about a boy who marries a girl suffering from leucoderma after reading her book, *Mahashweta*. In another story, she has mentioned about insensitive people who can spend on their housewarming but not for the victims of Gujarat earthquake.

She talks about her teacher who said that, "the greatest joy to a teacher is to produce students better than him". About an uneducated lady who sees the positive side of life and stays happy, and there is another one in which a shopkeeper adjusts the price of his wares as per the financial status of the customer. She also mentions about a lady who asks her who her ghost writer is. She talks about the facilities for women in Stockholm, about Alfred Nobel and the Nobel Prize and about the plight of unwed mothers in India and abroad.

She writes about the misuse of the telephone by the kids, about the biased nature of a lady when it concerns her daughter and daughter-in-law, about how people took advantage of an earthquake to set up house, about how a poor fisher boy contributes whatever he can for his family. She talks about how money can change the relationship between a husband and wife and about the different ways in which people look at life. In the last story she has mentioned about how different people express their gratitude; some say thank you and some do not even acknowledge you.

Exploring the elements of the post-structuralist thought in Sudha Murty's *Wise and Otherwise: A Salute to Life* can rejuvenate the pessimistic people's life into the optimistic one. The indelible imprints of the encounters Murty had with people during her travels and lifetime has been delineated in the beautiful manner by her in the book. It has been translated into several Indian languages. The present chapter is an attempt to study the events from the book through which one can learn how the two sets of the binaries in the discourse are equal in status and none is privileged to the other. With the endorsement to Saussure's (proponent of structuralism) concept of Binary Opposition (Black/White), Derrida, French philosopher, cleverly eschews the privilege of any set of binaries and posits that one element has its firm existence in the discourse only because of the existence of the opposite of it. Post-structuralism is most clearly distinct from structuralism in its rejection of structuralism's tendency to seek simple, universal and hierarchical structures.

Post-structuralists challenge the structuralist claim to be a critical metalanguage by which all text can be translated. Instead, they pursue an infinite play of signifiers and do not attempt to impose or privilege one reading of them over another. Jacques Derrida, Roland Barthes (after the publication of the essay *Death of the Author* in 1968), Michel Foucault and the philosopher Jean-Francois are the key figures of Post-structuralism. Basically, Jacques Derrida's paper on *Structure, Sign and Play in the Discourse of the Human Sciences* delivered in Johns Hopkins University is considered as the origin of Post-structuralism. It, unlike structuralism (originated from linguistics) has its origin from philosophy and from there it inherits the habit of skepticism and intensifies it.

A Summary

Here we are presenting the summary of stories in sequence.

A student who wants to study got sponsored when a woman read his story in newspaper. She sent him money for the class. When she sent him money again, he returned Rs. 300 saying that for two months he didn't visit Bellary because of holidays and strike in college. His honesty impressed the woman because even though he was poor, he didn't let go of his honesty.

A woman was sent to village for site checking. A guy, known to be the only well - read person of village, feels shy after getting a compliment from that woman. He invites her home for tea, where she praises his child. But then he gets caught in his own lie for he boasts of getting a gold medal in the college. Apparently, the woman turns out to be his batch mate and had won the gold medal whch he had falsely claimed.

An old man teaches the chapter of humility, of give and take, even when he himself had nothing much to offer. His ancestors' philosophy and beliefs made him do so.

In another story, the narrator asks her daughter-in-law to go pay her condolences to the neighbour as the lady of that house had passed away. But after ten days when the daughter-in-law of the narrator goes and visits the family again, she finds them in a cheerful mood. The daughter-in-law is angry at the narrator for having been forced to visit the house of the deceased woman.

A doctor who shares anecdotes to keep his class engrossed in his lectures gives the best advice to his daughter – a death in the hospital is just another death for the medicos, but a permanent loss for the family members. So one not make fun   of it.

A village in Kalahandi where people are ruled by the Kind, they use the ancient barter system in their daily dealings and think that the East India Company still rules them, feel that they don't own anything in the world.

An old man was left in an old age home by his son. The son left him in the care of an NGO worker, stating that the old man was alone and had no one to look after him. But when the old man dies, the son appears claiming stake to the old man's money. The NGO worker feels bad for the old man and laterteh son feels bad for his own act.

A guy talks about people who simply enjoy festivals without knowing its history, and then he talk about how orphanages are helped by raising funds. Then he eavesdrops on women who talk about the merits and demerits of software engineers. He later comes to know they are marriage brokers.

A woman, working in a city, at a time when telegram was a means of urgent communication, is scared on receiving news about a death in the family. She rushes home to find it is her cousins father who had passed away and not her own father. She feels relieved without realizing that someone had lost a loved one.

An old man approaches Sudha Murty and requests her to buy books from him for her library project. He doesn't know Sudha Murty, and he assumes that the woman whom he is talking to is just another employee. He tries to impress her by stating that he knows Sudha and Narayan Murthy and they have bought books from him earlier too. Sudha rejects him saying that if he was honest, she would have thought of buying, but now even if he gives them to her for free, she will not accept them.

A pessimist friend who sees negative in everything, left for Bombay. When they meet after a few years, the friend's outlook has changed completely. On enquiring, he says an encounter with a beggar changed his life. The beggar, despite not having anything, seemed to enjoy life to the fullest, while the friend was sad all the time.

Author narrated the story of Rani Jhansi and her courage to two ignorant youngsters and they listened to her talk carefully.

A passenger sitting beside the author during one of her travels gave her a tough time with her questions. When the author said that her head has started aching, the passenger, who turned out to be a salesgirl of a balm company, quickly gave her a balm bottle.

Heartwrenching story about the fate of girls after they get married. A married woman was admitted to the hospital with severe burn injuries; the doctors were told that the stove burst when she was cooking. In reality, the in-laws burnt her because she was pregnant with a girl child. As the author is consoling the girls mother, the girl dies.

Author and friends at a get together exchange their experiences; the one who was bright and beautiful is now become opposite of it, and the one who was mediocre had become a business woman. Things changed because beautiful and bright didn't take decision for themselves but mediocre did and was successful.

Independence Day is just a holiday for us. We fail to remember the saga of our heroes.

Earlier people were good and easy going and listened to advice of the elders and behaved maturely, but today they are altogether different and arrogant, behave improperly even when they are wrong.

Sometimes not shawls and garlands but just a Jasmine string given with respect is important to us; author feels the same. When her hard work was credited to some politician who was just there to get honour without lifting a finger for the hospital they build in village, the author didn't mind. She felt elated when a woman showed her appreciation by giving the author a Jasmine string.

When the author spotted leprosy stricken women who are shunned by the society, and are so poor that they don't have a proper cover for their bodies, the author gifts all these women a sari as she feels sorry for them.

The author gave money to a woman with terminal illness for her treatment. On her death bed, the ill woman thinks of donating the money that is left with her so that other patients can be treated. She passes away, and requests her brother to fulfill her last wish. The author feels proud of helping honest people.

A boy backs out of the relationship when he comes to know that the girl he loves is suffering from leucoderma. But after reading the author's book, he changes his mind and marries the girl.

Author visit's a friend's house warming party in 2002. After holy puja the talks shift to Gujarat earthquake 2002. She feels sad that no one is ready to help the earthquake affected people but will not shy away from showing off their wealth at housewarming parties and other functions.

One must respect one's teacher wherever one meets them because they have taught us and shaped us.

Every generation has grouses against the next generation, but these can be solved if we communicate - like author does with her son.

Author feels pity for women who are sex workers and want to get away from this profession.

Two different women, two different personalities but actual difference is about thought processing - one wants to gain experience, the other doesn't care at all.

Difference of rich and poor differentiated by a fruit seller through work and dowry related issues.

Difference between philanthropists back in 20th century and now a days, earlier people didn't advertise about the help they gave to other, now people want acknowledgement for there donations.

Woman must be well educated - not mere bookish knowledge but practical life experiences too. They should be self-dependent and have authority over their decisions and stand firm on that.

Jealous and self-centred people are dangerous, they make negative remarks without caring what one feels by their remarks. And their relationship deteriorates.

Country where goddesses are preached are at the bottom in a survey about respecting women but the Scandanavian country Norway, Sweden and Denmark respect their women more than anything.

Few sages are true Sanyasis, rest are all fraudsters and demi gods who mock and ruin life of many. A true Sanyasi become a leader and plays a role accordingly.

Negative and positive views of the people in author's column in newspaper.

Idea of Nobel prize is to recognise the help provided to mankind by people who work selflessly.

Unwed mother is a curse in the Indian family.

Marriage of Friend's daughter who is going to US and doesn't have anything to give in dowry except for the tickets to US. How time changes and changes things.

Confidence of a guy few decades back to learn and understand computer and today's youth is different.

Telephone and how it is abused by children in author's Friend's house by his daughter upsets the situation in their life because they cannot control their needs and desires.

Hypocrisy of people in the same house - like what daughter did in her in-laws house is good, but what their daughter-in-law did it's wrong, why?

Difference between the educated friend's son who is waiting to join a software job to earn big money and doesn't want to settle for less, whereas a child wakes up at 5 in the morning and works till 11pm to earn 5 rupees to buy the stuff. He can't splurge as the pay is low.

Difference between teachers who lead by good and bad example, at one time teachers treated their students like family, now they are exploited.

Difference in people's thought process as people want to be treated like humans and not mere machine and children should be treated as per their age.

A friend who never spent money on unworthy things, after retirement splurged, and another man used his wealth for philanthropic work.

Money changes people - makes them arrogant.

Mental health deteriorating because love is missing in relationships, torture and taunts make a person mad, money can't make you happy for a long time.

Summing Up

To conclude, it is a collection of around fifty one short stories, a tapestry of human character, behavior and attitudes. The stories are simple and filled with emotions. Here we get to see the real neglected interiors of India that needs immediate help. We understand a new definition and meaning for the much-used term 'Women Empowerment'. The philanthropy world which plays the role of a fundraiser is an eye-opener for most of us. Sudha Murty has written these stories to throw the light on some strong values that still exist in our society. There are lessons of values such as honesty, compassion, hard work, giving back to the society, empathizing with the people who are in need, enjoying the beauty of every minute of life, never late to learn to be more human, the significance of being an Indian and what not!

References

Murty, Sudha (2002), *Wise and Otherwise: A Salute to Life*, East West Books Pvt. Ltd (Madras)

Murty, Sudha (2006), *Wise and Otherwise: A Salute to Life*, Penguin Random House India

3

Dollar Bahu

"What separates old from the young is experience and patience."- Sudha Murty

Indian writing in English has reached global acclaim in the hands of various embryonic new writers of this contemporary era. In recent times numerous writers have contributed to the growth and development of Indian English literature through their artistic portrayal under various literary genres. Sudha Murty--who blooms in this category of modern women writer--contributes to Indian English literature on a large scale. She captures the true spirit of Indian culture in all her creative works. She tries to incorporate many Indian mythologies too in her literary works.

Her fiction *Dollar Bahu* apprehends realistically the Indian culture and she attempts to bring out the hardships of immigrant marriage experience in the milieu of Indian background through her characters.

It is apt to mention here that due to the popularity, the novel *Dollar Bahu* was converted into a television series. The story portrays the struggle of a middle-class family to graduate into an upper-class one through their son in the USA. Besides, as the title refers, the series was shot in both India as well as in the United States. In addition, when the serial's shooting began in the USA, the 11 September incident occurred, leaving the entire team of 'Dollar Bahu' devastated.

It is to be noted that the story is about two daughters-in-law of a family, one from America and the other one from India. Now, how their mother-in-law treats them (Rupees and Dollar) is uncovered. The story is more of the mother-in-law who thinks that her American daughter-in-law (dollar bahu) is better than her counterpart in India, since she lives in the land of dreams, USA. Henceforth, she desires to live with her son in America. However, when she lives a year or so in America, she realises that the Indians living there face the same problems and challenges as those living in India. She realises that "grass always looks greener on the other side". And when she comes back to India, she shows immense love to the daughter-in-law whom she treated like a trash. Finally after getting a slap on feelings by her dollar bahu, Gouramma understands the fact that may be dollar can remove the poverty from one's life, but family is much more important than money.

Evidently a morality tale about human greed.

At its heart this is a book that explores greed, prejudice and respect (or lack thereof) for other people. It dissects the differences in values and customs of both America and India, albeit rather simplistically. But this is not a novella that is interested in nuances or shades of grey: it is completely black and white and as blunt as a spoon.

At its most core it paints America as a rich but soulless country where family ties and personal connections are not important; and India as impoverished and slightly backward but where the traditional values of family and marriage are sacrosanct.

Yet the message of the story, neatly summarised by Shamanna (who has never left India), does ring true:

"… nothing is absolute in life. America has a set of advantages and disadvantages. Similarly, India has its own. You cannot have the best of both worlds. If you have a choice, choose a country and accept it with its pluses and minuses and live happily there. Staying in America and dreaming of an Indian way of life, or living in India and expecting an American way of life--both are roads to grief."

Dollar Bahu is wholly predictable, the characterisation is poor and one-dimensional (the nasty mother-in-law, the greedy daughter, the stuck up daughter-in-law, the wise father and so on) and a little too reliant on cultural stereotypes to be anything other than a light read. It feels like it's aimed at uneducated Indians, warning them that America is not the paradise they might expect it to be--or perhaps I'm simply reading too much into it.

Thus goes the story. Shamanna, a teacher, and Gouramma, a home maker, are a middle - class and middle - aged couple. They are blessed with two sons, Chandru, an engineer with a private firm, and Girish, a clerk in a bank, and a daughter, Surabhi. Shamanna believes in values, but Gouramma is after riches.

Chandru goes to Dharwad on a project and meets Vinuta (Vinu for short) in whose house he stays as a paying guest. She is an orphan, looked after by a well-meaning distant relative, a student, a singer, and versatile in domestic chores. For Chandru, it is love at first sight, but his main sight is on bigger things, like making it big in the U.S.A. He doesn't tell her of his feelings for her, even when he's recalled to Bangalore only to be sent on a project to the U.S.A.

Chandru lives his 'Dollar Dreams', and enjoys the material comforts that the U.S. offers, but realises the need to have a family after a while. So he writes to Vinu to ask whether she's interested in him.

Fate has something else in store- meanwhile the relative of Vinu's in whose care she lived in Dharwad, passes away, forcing her to shift to Bangalore. It is an emotional moment for her to leave the home in which she grew up, but it is heartening that she's not disposing it off.

In Bangalore, Vinu works in the same school as Shamanna, and bumps into Girish one day. He develops a liking for the girl and expresses it to his father who is also in favour of the alliance. Meanwhile, Chandru's 'love letter' returns to him undelivered (there's no one residing in that home, right?) and with its return ends Chandru's love for Vinu.

Chandru's visit to the U.S. enables them to have a first floor in their modest home. But that does not deter Gouramma from hoping for a 'status' compliance from the bride.

Since Chandru does not plan to return till he gets a green card, he doesn't mind his younger brother getting married earlier.

Though Gouramma insists that bride's side approach them first, Shamanna arranges it; Vinuta has no great hopes either, so she's willing to marry a clerk. The moment Vinu and Girish see each other, they are willing to marry each other but Gouramma throws in a spanner – of a grand wedding – and even suggests the disposing of the house at Dharwad. Shamanna intervenes and lets the boy and the girl decide.

Girish, who has taken on the complexion and attitude of his father, agrees to a simple marriage but warns Vinu that her mother, though affectionate, can act tough at times.

The wedding photos make Chandru uneasy and jealous, but, in due course, he digests the fact.

Gouramma likes her daughter-in-law, until her elder son returns, that is. The concern of Gouramma and Surabhi over the gifts that Chandru brings on his return is well-presented.

Suddenly, rich parents of eligible girls take notice of Gouramma. A shrewd property developer, Krishnappa, impresses Gouramma with a lavish display of gold, silver and diamonds at their farm house. This blurs Gouramma from the reality that Jamuna, Krishnappa's daughter, was rejected by better looking and well-settled grooms because of her plain looks. The girl makes sure this alliance is not lost by being extremely amiable with Surabhi. Gouramma is very much in favour of this alliance. Chandru's rendezvous with Jamuna is more like a business negotiation.

Once the alliance is finalised, Vinu is relegated to the background, only meant to take care of the household, while Gouramma and Surabhi are all over the place. Chandru remembers Vinu's favourite colour and buys her an aquamarine saree with a pink border costing a huge sum, despite his mother's antagonism to it.

The mother-in-law gives up two of her gold bangles to give an expensive present to her 'Dollar Bahu', Jamuna. This is the beginning of the differentiation that Vinu is set to undergo.

During the wedding, Girish and Vinu work hard, while Gouramma handles money. When Chandru leaves for the U.S., the elder daughter-in-law makes an excuse and goes back to her parents' place and turns up only to intimate the news of her departure to the Land of Opportunity.

Vinuta subsequently becomes a forced listener to all the lavish praise of her mother-in-law for Jamuna, which hurts her. Girish takes it lightly, so she gets hurt further.

The dual standards of Gouramma while being on the hunt for a boy for Surabhi (if the boy were the only son, the in-laws would stay permanently with them, and therefore the boy was undesirable) and those of Surabhi herself (she can pass time with some neighbourhood boy, but she can marry only a rich boy) are well described. The efforts of Girish and Vinuta in preventing Surabhi from getting married to a boy having a live-in girlfriend are not appreciated by the mother-daughter duo. On top of it, Gouramma and Surabhi take out their anger on Vinu-- she is blamed as the one creating a ruckus in the family.

The date of Surabhi's wedding is fixed to suit the timing of Jamuna's convenience. Alas, poor Vinuta is packed off to Dharwad for her confinement, all because Chandru's contribution to the wedding was higher.

Jamuna lavishes Surabhi with a lot of sarees at the latter's wedding, which Vinu is unable to. In addition, Vinuta's services to her mother-in-law in a case of suspected cancer are quickly forgotten because the lump is benign!

By the time Jamuna is expecting a child, Vinu is only expected to take instructions and no longer recognised as a human.

The prayers of the mother-in-law for the safe delivery of Jamuna hurt Vinu further. Nothing was done by Gouramma when she was in the family way!

Gouramma is very excited to be in the U.S. for Jamuna's delivery. She makes some friends of the friends of Chandru and her conversations with them on their experiences open her mind to progressive thinking. A baby girl is born, and pampered by her grandma, who slowly realises that the 'Dollar Bahu' is only a pretender and had no genuine concern for her. The fact that the sarees presented to Surabhi for her wedding were used sarees comes as a shock to Gouramma; the last straw on the camel's back comes when Gouramma overhears her 'Dollar Bahu' tell her friends that by bringing in the mother-in-law, she got a cheap baby sitter who took good care of her daughter. She also makes a reference to the fact that the loving Vinu is looked down upon.

By the time Gouramma is back in India, she realises that Vinu, Girish and their son had gone to Dharwad. Vinu's health had deteriorated because of the double standards, so the understanding father-in-law had advised them to take a transfer.

The story of a betrothed groom who dumps his bride to get married to an American Indian, of the Bangalore doctor who double-charges Chandru since he is from the U.S. and of others who survived the difficulties in U.S. to become successful are interwoven with the main plot. 'Dollar Bahu' or not, it is very common to find mothers-in-law showing favouritism towards a richer daughter-in-law or towards a daughter vis-à-vis a daughter-in-law.

Inner Conflict of Leading Female Characters in *Dollar Bahu*

As is evident, the characters of Sudha Murty's novels are drawn from everyday lives. The attitude and trait of her characters is highly influenced by social conformity, where the individual's behaviour has been paramount from the early stages of personality development.

Every human being is a microcosm in a larger society. The nature of every individual varies highly with respect to his personality. Even a very normal person, when brought under the microscope of psychology, opens up a world of new interpretations.

In the Indian context when a woman gets married, she marries not only the individual but a whole family consisting of numerous relationships like, mother-in-law, father-in-law, sister-in-law, brother-in-law and so on. Sudha Murty silently perceives everything minutely and delicately. She explores the different roles of woman as that of a wife, mother-in-law and sister-in-law.

Dollar-Bahu is a beautiful portrayal of a middle class family residing at Jayanagar, Bengaluru. The novel highlights the fact that family love, affection and bonding are more important than money.

Basically the story is set in two countries, the first half in India, in which is explored the sensibility of the protagonist Vinuta, within the framework of the disintegrating relationship in her household, due to the blinded passion developed by her mother-in-law for the 'Dollar'. The second part of the story is set in America, when Vinuta's mother-in-law, Gouramma, visits her older son Chandru. On the American stage, Sudha Murty has successfully interwoven stories of many Indians living in America, juxtaposing one story with another. As Gouramma meets every character she matures inwardly, and finally understands that family bond holds more riches than 'Dollar'.

It is worth-mentioning here that the main focus of the novel is on the interesting twists it holds. As the plot unfolds, the twists are disentangled one after the other lending a lot of unexpected surprises. The relation between Vinuta and Chandru is snapped abruptly when Chandru is sent to America. Vinuta's peaceful life at her home in Dharwad catapults when Bheemanna, Vinuta's uncle dies of an unexpected heart attack. Vinuta relocates to her aunt's house in Bangalore and joins the same school in which Shamanna (Chandru's father) teaches. Vinuta and Girish, Chandru's brother are united in a wedlock.

Chandru returns to India after a good six years. He becomes the eligible bachelor and a wedding is arranged for him with Jamuna, the only daughter of an affluent property developer Krishnappa. They return to America soon after the wedding.

Gouramma has trouble in coping with and handling the societal stress resulting in the fear of unacceptance. She always dreamed of diamonds, gold and silver, jewellery, cars, a big house, servants etc. and thought that these were the tickets to help her move in the elite circle. She found her desires getting fulfilled through Chandru's dollars. Between Jamuna's dollars and Vinuta's selfless devotion, Gouramma finds favour with the dollar and ignores Vinuta's devotion and family bonding which actually is truly priceless. Vinuta bears the brunt of endless comparisons between her and 'Dollar Bahu'. She starts withering physically and mentally at these constant attacks meted out at her.

Gouramma then gets a chance to go to America to live with her son for a year, she opens her eyes to the faults of Jamuna and realizes that Jamuna is basically a very selfish person. She gets to meet a lot of Indian families settled in America and this helps her to change her opinion on life she had till then. She understands the affection and devotion Vinuta holds for the family in contrast with Jamuna's selfishness. Money does speak honey but it also corrupts the way people look at each other and has the power to tear the family apart.

Vinuta becomes very depressed as Gouramma's arrival draws near. She begins to resent the word 'dollar'. The continuous erosion of family values impairs the bond Vinuta has with her mother-in-law.

Seeing the misery of Vinuta, Shamanna finally decides to send Vinuta and Girish to Dharwad. The decision comes as a surprise for Vinuta. Shamanna reasons that the decision would make Girish independent, assertive and confident just as Chandru has become after going to America.

Vinuta and Girish leave for Dharwad to live there on the insistence of Shamanna, before Gouramma reaches Bangalore. Though upset that they have left without her permission, she understands that it is time to leave her children to their independence.

Analysing the three major characters, we can appropriate them to Karen Horney's idea of neurosis and psycho-analysis involving inner conflicts.

Gouramma is in a desperate need for acceptance in the elite circle. When this aspiration does not get met, it pops up as anxiety, anger etc. and Vinuta becomes her soft target and wields control over her. This arises due to the neurotic need to have control and power over others. She is obsessed with the thoughts of becoming rich and sees Chandru's job as the perfect gateway to acquire this. Her experience in America greatly influences her personality. She realizes that she is treated with no self-respect and is at the loss of cognitive abilities which was her forte while at Bangalore. This new analysis of herself changes her opinions and perceptions of life and brings about a potential self-realization. In the three ways of neurotic needs proposed by Karen Horney, Gouramma is seen as moving against people because she is bossy, demanding and sometimes even cruel.

Jamuna is seen as moving away from people her because of her indifferent attitude. She manipulates Gouramma. She wishes to be accepted, praised and worshipped and flaunts her wealth at them to mute them against her shortcomings of not respecting or spending time with her wedded family. She thinks that she is entitled to special privileges and has a false pride based not on reality but on a distorted and idealized view of self. She can also be seen to be suffering from hyper competitiveness. She is cold and aloof not only to Gouramma and Vinuta but towards Chandru as well.

On the other hand, Vinuta starts developing inner conflicts after the wedding of Jamuna. She struggles to cope with and control her interpersonal issues that arise because of the comparison between Jamuna – The Dollar Bahu and she, the simpleton. She is emotionally disturbed by the fears and tries to find compromising strategies for her fears. But she wallows all the more in depression. She becomes a kind of neurotic feeling isolated, helpless and afraid. She worries that she would become hostile not only to her mother-in-law but her whole family. She is finally liberated from these emotional conflicts by her father-in-law's decision to send her away to her childhood home at Dharwad, the place she is emotionally attached to and has a lot of childhood memories. She is seen to move towards people because she seeks affirmation, acceptance, approval and love from her family members.

Focus on Acculturating Experience

Sudha Murty--who writes in the backdrop of Indian literature--brings out the element of Indian culture in all possible ways. Her fiction *Dollar Bahu* traces the immigrant experience in the land of the US through various characters. Gouramma--one of the lead characters of the novel--visits America, feeling so happy for experiencing and witnessing her long term goal in life. Through the eyes of Gouramma, Sudha Murty brings various immigrant experiences which in turn teach many life lessons in the backdrop of Indian culture.

Chandru's Fear in Raising His Daughter

In fact, Gouramma experienced cultural shock under various circumstances. For instance, once Chandru was worrying about his difficulty in raising his child in the land of a foreign nation. He expressed as, "when they are young, they mingle with other kids, talk in their accent, and feel very proud. But when they behave like American teenagers, we get upset. At times, I think about my daughter and get scared." He brooded over his mental struggle in raising his newborn child, which he associated with the difficulty encountered by one of his friend's named Venkant in America. Venkant's daughter was experiencing a teenage problem due to which their family got shattered into pieces without real happiness. Gouramma was shocked to know about the difficulty in raising the children and agonized inwardly after empathizing and realizing the difficulty endured by her son in raising his daughter.

Radhakrishna and Savitri were worried exactly about the same thing. What people may think if their daughter finds her own life partner troubled them so much, so they arranged a quick marriage for Shama. Nevertheless, Shama's marital life was broken because the groom was interested in amassing the benefits and material wealth that her parents owned rather than spreading real love and happiness. After her broken relationship with her husband, her live-in-relationship with a Brazilian boyfriend tormented Gourammma even more. Shama retaliated, "from now on I want to live the way I want. Don't you dare interfere! " Gouramma was baffled and felt a strange fear thinking about her grand-daughter and her future life in a foreign land after knowing about Shama's current situation and the problems encountered by her parents in the foreign land.

Life Struggle of Shama

As already stated, Gouramma experienced a cultural shock from the life of the immigrant couple--Radhakrishna and Savitri. They arranged marriage for Shama--first daughter--at the age of twenty-one. Savitri expresses as "we were afraid that she would get into wrong company and find a boyfriend or some such thing" . So they decided to marry their daughter by finding a guy from an Indian background. All forms of culture exhibit unique ways and value systems that aid and affect individuals in their perception and reaction to different life circumstances.

Broken Marital Life of Tara

Gouramma happened to meet Tara during her stay in America. Her life story was yet another shock for her. Tara was married to Ramesh and she came to the US after her wedding only. Her parents sold their property to give her a lavish wedding. But after her wedding, she was astonished to know the fact that Ramesh was already married. Ramesh married her because of family pressure without revealing his marital status. Gouramma related Tara's incident with her daughter's married life and she was worried about the unknown humiliation which she might encounter in her life through the life of her grandchildren.

Melancholy of Asha Patil

Yet another character with fragile relationship, life story of Asha Patil also brought cultural shock to Gouramma. Asha Patil was married to Sathish Patil by her parents thinking that he was a great businessman. But he owned a *bhel-puri* cart in reality and she was assaulted very cruelly by his family members. Later, Asha Patil sank into a great depression and she struggled a lot to overcome her difficult situation. Her broken marriage was indeed a great shock for Gouramma because she thought life in America is so luxurious and comfortable than in India. But after witnessing Asha's struggle for survival she understood the difficulty and the intricacies involved behind it. After witnessing so many disparities, Gouramma was perplexed and worried and she found it very difficult to digest the hard realities of life in a foreign land.

In a nutshell, Gouramma experienced so many intricacies in a foreign nation through the eyes of various immigrant characters during her short stay in America. As the proverb goes 'The grass is always greener on the other side' Gouramma longed for the life in Dollar nation and she wished that all her sons and daughter settle in the US. She realized the fact that life always looks green on the other side and finally valued the importance of her own land. Gouramma's self - realization because of her short stay in America resulted in her understanding the true situation and it resulted in forming a good relationship with her family members irrespective of their earnings in dollars or rupees.

Summing Up

Dollar Bahu is a literary panopticon of Indian values which surveys the changing perspectives of Indian people due to the fascination of the westernization. Values are the indispensible phenomenon of human life which must be cherished to survive humanity and individuality. The significance and the subjugation of Indian values are explicated by Sudha Murty through the characters in *Dollar Bahu* with an appeal to the Indian people to respect and cherish the rich Indian values.

References

"Dollar Bahu survives WTC attack", *Screen India*, 21 September 2001.

"Sudha Murthy's 'Dollar Bahu' on Zee," India FM. 2001, Archived from the original on 4 April 2008.

"The million-dollar name behind Dollar Bahu", *Tribune India*, 30 September 2001.

Friedman, H. S., & Schustack, M. W. (2015). Personality: Classic Theories and Modern Research (6th ed.). Boston, MA: Pearson/Allyn and Bacon.

Furnham, Adrian (2010), Culture Shock: Literature Review, Personal Statement, and Relevance for the South Pacific. Journal of Pacific Rim Psychology. Vol. 4, No. 2. pp. 87–94.

Horney, Karen (1942), Self-Analysis. New York: W.W Norton and Company, Inc.

Horney, Karen (1945), Our Inner Conflicts: A Constructive Theory of Neurosis. New York: W.W. Norton and Company, Inc.

Horney, Karen (1950), Neurosis and Human Growth: The Struggle toward Self-Realization. New York: W.W. Norton and Company, Inc, 1950.

Lebron, Antonio (2013), What is Culture? Merit Research Journal of Education and Review. Vol. 1. No. 6. pp. 126-132.

Moufakkir, Omar (2013), Culture shock, what culture shock? Conceptualizing culture unrest in intercultural tourism and assessing its effect on tourists' perceptions and travel propensity, *Tourist Studies*, Vol. 13, No. 3, pp. 322–340.

Murty, Sudha (2007), *Dollar Bahu*, New Delhi: Penguin Books India.

Schultz, D. P., & Schultz, S. E. (2012), *Theories of Personality* (10th ed.). Belmont, CA: Wadsworth/Cengage Learning.

4

How I taught My Grandmother to Read and Other Stories

"With my experience in life, I want to tell you that having good relationships, compassion and peace of mind is much more important than achievements, awards, degrees or money."- Sudha Murty

How I Taught My Grandmother to Read is a fictional short story written by prolific author Sudha Murty. This story was published in the book *How I Taught My Grandmother to Read and Other Stories* in the year 2004 by Penguin Books, India.

Here in this chapter we will present an analytical description of the story and other stories contained in the collection.

Summary of the Work

The author recalls her childhood memories. When the author was a girl of about twelve, she used to stay in a village in North Karnataka with her grandparents. Since the transport system was not very good in those days, they used to get the morning newspaper not until the afternoon. The weekly magazine used to come in a day late. All of them would wait eagerly for the bus, which arrived with the newspapers, weekly magazine and the post.

At that time, Triveni was a very popular writer in the Kannada language and all the village people would wait eagerly for the weekly magazine 'Karmaveera', where one of her novel *Kashi Yatre* was appearing as a serial. It was the story of an old lady and her earnest desire to go to Kashi or Banares or Varanasi, where she wished to worship Lord Vishweshwara to attain ultimate blessings. But finally, the old lady sacrifices all her savings for the marriage of a young, poor girl, who falls in love but there was no money for her wedding. So the old lady gave away all her savings.

Impressed by the plot of *Kashi Yatre*, the author's grandmother Krishtakka would listen to the story as her granddaughter (the author) read the episodes to her. She was so touched with the story that later, she could repeat the entire text by heart. She never went to school and so, she couldn't read it by herself. Afterwards, she used to join her friends at the temple park and would discuss the latest episodes [because Triveni was a popular writer and common people could relate to the complex psychological problems in her stories]. She could relate to the protagonist of the story.

After she returns from enjoying a week-long wedding with her cousins, she finds her grandmother in tears. When she asks her what the matter was, her grandmother narrates the story of her life to the author. She expresses her grief of getting married very early and therefore not getting a chance to receive an education. She explains that while the author was away, *Karmaveera* came in as usual. But she couldn't read a single alphabet and felt very embarrassed, helpless and dependent. After this, she firmly decides that she will learn to read the Kannada alphabet from the next day onwards and keep the day of Saraswati Puja as the deadline. That day she would be able to read a novel by herself.

As a result, from the next day the author started her tuition and found her grandmother to be a very intelligent and hardworking student. She diligently did her homework and slowly learnt to read, repeat, write and recite.

When the Dussehra festival came as usual, the writer secretly bought *Kashi Yatre* which had been published as a novel by that time. The author got a gift of cotton material from her grandmother. Then suddenly her grandmother bent down and touched her feet. The author found this as extremely bizarre since elders never touch the feet of youngsters and thought that her grandmother had broken the rules of the tradition. But in response to that, her grandmother replied that she was touching the feet of a Guru (teacher), not her 12-year-old granddaughter as it was the custom that a teacher should be respected, irrespective of gender and age. She explained that her granddaughter was a very caring and loving teacher who taught her so well that she could easily read any novel confidently. This way, the author had helped her grandmother to become independent.

How I taught my grandmother to read shows the curious desire of a sixty-two year old grandmother namely, Krishtakka to learn Kannada language. The old lady firmly believed that reading enriched one's personality. She thought of learning to read independently without external help. She started learning alphabet from her granddaughter Sudha and within a stipulated time, she learned reading and writing on her own. Story showed the unshakable determination of an old lady. She told Sudha, "For a good cause if you are determined, you can overcome any obstacle. I will work harder than anybody, but I will do it. For learning there is no age bar."

The story ends as the author gives the gift to her grandmother and her grandmother is able to read the title *Kashi Yatre* by Triveni and the publisher's name aloud all by herself.

Theme

It is pertinent to note that in *How I Taught My Grandmother to Read* by Sudha Murty we have the theme of love, independence, desperation and happiness. Narrated in the first person by an unnamed woman the story is a retrospective look at the narrator's life with her grandmother and how she taught her grandmother to read. It also becomes clear to the reader after reading the story that the narrator and the grandmother love each other very much. Though Avva (the grandmother) left school early she makes up for her inability to read by giving so much love to her granddaughter; a love that is reciprocated by the narrator. It also becomes clear to the reader that Avva longs to be able to read. So much so that she asks the narrator to help her begin to read, a task which results in being successful.

The theme of independence is also evident in the story. Avva believes that should she be able to read she will be more independent and not as reliant on the narrator to read her stories from the magazine. Reading today is taken for granted and it can be difficult to imagine there are those who cannot read but due to Avva's circumstances she never learned to read. She was orphaned young and married young and family life took precedence. It is only now through old age and desperation that Avva feels it is the right time to start reading.

There may also be some symbolism in the story which might be important. The fact that Avva cannot read may be Murty's way of suggesting that some people slip through the education net, that some people are forgotten about when they cannot read. Since the grandmother is sixty-two years old, Murty might also be symbolically suggesting that it is never too late for a person to learn how to read. Especially from someone they love, the narrator. It may also be the case that the narrator despite originally laughing at Avva is the right person to help her grandmother. Murty, by having someone who loves her, may be suggesting that Avva and the narrator are fine bedfellows because they love one another so much.

The end of the story is interesting because Murty appears to be exploring the theme of happiness. The narrator successfully teaches Avva to read and she is able to read the novel that she wants to. No longer is Avva reliant on her granddaughter in order for her to read her stories. She has successfully learnt the alphabet and been able to understand exactly what she is reading. Thanks to the narrator's hard work and Avva's desire, Avva is able to read without hesitation. She has become independent of others.

Let's have a reading of the text of the story.

Text of How I Taught My Grandmother to Read

"When I was a girl of about twelve, I used to stay in a village in north Karnataka with my grandparents. Those days, the transport system was not very good, so we used to get the morning paper only in the afternoon. The weekly magazine used to come one day late. All of us would wait eagerly for the bus, which used to come with the papers, weekly magazines and the post.

At that time, Triveni was a very popular writer in the Kannada language. She was a wonderful writer. Her style was easy to read and very convincing. Her stories usually dealt with complex psychological problems in the lives of ordinary people and were always very interesting. Unfortunately for Kannada literature, she died very young. Even now, after forty years, people continue to appreciate her novels.

One of her novels, called *Kashi Yatre*, was appearing as a serial in the Kannada weekly *Karmaveera* then. It is the story of an old lady and her ardent desire to go to Kashi or Varanasi. Most Hindus believe that going to Kashi and worshipping Lord Vishweshvara is the ultimate *punya*. This old lady also believed in this, and her struggle to go there was described in that novel. In the story there was also a young orphan girl who falls in love but there was no money for the wedding. In the end, the old lady gives away all her savings without going to Kashi. She says, 'The happiness of this orphan girl is more important than worshipping Lord Vishweshwara at Kashi.'

My grandmother, Krishtakka, never went to school so she could not read. Every Wednesday the magazine would come and I would read the next episode of this story to her. During that time she would forget all her work and listen with the greatest concentration. Later, she could repeat the entire text by heart. My grandmother too never went to Kashi, and she identified herself with the novel's protagonist. So more than anybody else she was the one most interested in knowing what happened next in the story and used to insist that I read the serial out to her.

After hearing what happened next in *Kashi Yatre*, she would join her friends at the temple courtyard where we children would also gather to play hide and seek. She would discuss the latest episode with her friends. At that time, I never understood why there was so much of debate about the story.

Once I went for a wedding with my cousins to the neighbouring village. In those days, a wedding was a great event. We children enjoyed ourselves thoroughly. We would eat and play endlessly, savouring the freedom because all the elders were busy. I went for a couple of days but ended up staying there for a week.

When I came back to my village, I saw my grandmother in tears. I was surprised, for I had never seen her cry even in the most difficult situations. What had happened? I was worried.

'Avva, is everything all right? Are you ok?'

I used to call her Avva, which means mother in the Kannada spoken in north Karnataka.

She nodded but did not reply. I did not understand and forgot about it. In the night, after dinner, we were sleeping in the open terrace of the house. It was a summer night and there was a full moon. Avva came and sat next to me. Her affectionate hands touched my forehead. I realized she wanted to speak. I asked her, 'What is the matter?'

'When I was a young girl I lost my mother. There was nobody to look after and guide me. My father was a busy man and got married again. In those days people never considered education essential for girls, so I never went to school. I got married very young and had children. I became very busy. Later I had grandchildren and always felt so much happiness in cooking and feeding all of you. At times I used to regret not going to school, so I made sure that my children and grandchildren studied well …'

I could not understand why my sixty-two-year-old grandmother was telling me, a twelve-year-old, the story of her life in the middle of the night. But I knew I loved her immensely and there had to be some reason why she was talking to me. I looked at her face. It was unhappy and her eyes were filled with tears. She was a good-looking lady who was usually always smiling. Even today I cannot forget the worried expression on her face. I leaned forward and held her hand.

'Avva, don't cry. What is the matter? Can I help you in any way?'

'Yes, I need your help. You know when you were away, Karmaveera came as usual. I opened the magazine. I saw the picture that accompanies the story of *Kashi Yatre* and I could not understand anything that was written. Many times I rubbed my hands over the pages wishing they could understand what was written. But I knew it was not possible. If only I was educated enough. I waited eagerly for you to return. I felt you would come early and read for me. I even thought of going to the village and asking you to read for me. I could have asked somebody in this village but I was too embarrassed to do so. I felt so very dependent and helpless.

We are well-off, but what use is money when I cannot be independent?'

I did not know what to answer. Avva continued.

'I have decided I want to learn the Kannada alphabets from tomorrow onwards. I will work very hard. I will keep Saraswati Pooja day during Dassara as the deadline. That day I should be able to read a novel on my own. I want to be independent.'

I saw the determination on her face. Yet I laughed at her.

'Avva, at this age of sixty-two you want to learn alphabets? All your hair are grey, your hands are wrinkled, you wear spectacles and you work so much in the kitchen…'

Childishly I made fun of the old lady. But she just smiled.

'For a good cause if you are determined, you can overcome any obstacle. I will work harder than anybody but I will do it. For learning there is no age bar.'

The next day onwards I started my tuition. Avva was a wonderful student. The amount of homework she did was amazing. She would read, repeat, write and recite. I was her only teacher and she was my first student. Little did I know then that one day I would become a teacher in Computer Science and teach hundreds of students.

The Dassara festival came as usual. Secretly I bought *Kashi Yatre* which had been published as a novel by that time. My grandmother called me to the puja place and made me sit down on a stool. She gave me a gift of a frock material. Then she did something unusual. She bent down and touched my feet. I was surprised and taken aback. Elders never touch the feet of youngsters. We have always touched the feet of God, elders and teachers. We consider that as a mark of respect. It is a great tradition but today the reverse had happened. It was not correct.

She said, 'I am touching the feet of a teacher, not my grand daughter; a teacher who taught me so well, with so much of affection that I can read any novel confidently in such a short period. Now I am independent. It is my duty to respect a teacher. Is it not written in our scriptures that a teacher should be respected, irrespective of the gender and age?'

I did return *namaskara* to her by touching her feet and gave my gift to my first student. She opened it and read immediately the title *Kashi Yatre* by Triveni and the publisher's name.

I knew then that my student had passed with flying colours."

Now we turn to other stories of the collection.

Books for at Least One Library describes the importance of books in the development of human character. Sudha Murty's grandfather was highly respected by the people around him for his knowledge. He used to say. "In this life everything perishes over a period of time. Whether it be diamond, beauty, gold or even land. Only one thing withstands - It is knowledge. The more you give the more you get." Story refers to the American billionaire who donated huge amount to the libraries in the state. He is remembered even after a century of his death, not for his wealth, but for his charitable love for books.

Salaam Abdul Kalam narrates the greatness of Kalam in reading the character of even an ordinary person correctly. He had realized the writing talent of SM through the reading of her articles in newspaper. The unassuming Kalam left an indelible mark on her personality. Kalam read the end part of any article first and if he found it interesting he would read the first part. Murty found a valid point in this habit and picked the same habit in reading and writing. Sudha Murty explained her habit of writing thus, "That was the best compliment I had ever received. When I write I always think of end first and then the beginning. Kalam seemed to have guessed it in no time."

Hassan's Attendance Problem shows the importance of good habits in life. Hassan, Murty's student in Engineering college scored a first class in every examination but was never punctual in attendance. In spite of his high intelligence and immaculate skills, no employer continued him for long because of his irregularity. As a result, when his classmates began to earn in millions, he had to make his living by marketing educational CDs at negligible prices. He knew that bad habits died hard but he was a helpless victim of his own nature. His teachers and Principal ignored his irregularities in the class but the competitive world outside was cruel and did not excuse him.

The Red Rice Granary puts forward the significance of bonafide intent with which one donates. Murty's grandmother always gave away quality rice to the needy hungry people who came to her door. The same grandmother, however, cooked raw red rice for the members of the family. Her grandmother told her, "Child whenever you want to give something to somebody, give the best in you, never the second best. That is what I have learned from life. God is not there in the temple, mosque or church. He is within the people. If you serve them with whatever you have, you have served God."

The Real Jewels narrates the importance of mother tongue and motherland in the life of an individual. Kultamma sent her son Aithappa from a forsaken village in South Karnataka to Bombay for his education. After completing his education, Aithappa started a chain of hotels in Bombay and earned millions of rupees. The old lady in Bombay became nostalgic of her people and her language. She returned home and started charity schools for the deprived section of the society there. Real jewel for her was not her son"s richness but it was his sacrifice for the people which was the real jewel.

A History Lesson on Teachers' Day tells about the condemnable ignorance of modern children about national heroes and national events. Murty was shocked to notice that her students did not know about the Independence Day, Republic Day and Martyr's Day. Students enjoyed the national holidays in trips and merrymaking. Sudha Murty could not restrain herself from explaining the significance of such days to the students who had come to the theatre to see the newly released movie. Her discussion with the boys and girls became a lesson in history.

Appro JRD is a pen painting of JRD Tata, the tycoon of Indian industries. Sudha Murty wrote a letter to JRD expressing her anguish and anger against the company's biased advertisement which had prohibited girls from applying for the Engineer's post. JRD not only took serious note of her letter but also selected her for the post. Sudha Murty writes about his compassion, generosity and foresight in this story. She was impressed by his humanitarian approach, his zeal for social work and his trusteeship attitude to his own wealth. She always kept JRD's photograph in her Infosys office to commemorate his constructive role in her life.

Heart of Gold is a story of compassionate policeman in New York. A policeman saw a destitute girl and her frail mother with a broken bowl begging in the crowded street. He was moved by the pitiable condition of a child girl and her mother. He gave away all the money that he had withdrawn from the bank to the girl. Few days passed when there was a newspaper report about the deceitful practices of the lady with a dying child. Policeman's son was angry with him for his thoughtless charity. The policeman calmly replied that he was happy that the child was healthy. The policeman did not mind the deceit as long as the child was in good condition. Instead of getting wild with the lady, his daughter's condition pleased him. Story shows the golden heart of a father in policeman.

Wedding in Russia describes a marriage convention in Russia. Marriage invariably took place on Saturday or Sunday in order to save working days. A newly wed couple was required to put on a military dress and visit a war memorial immediately after the marriage ceremony. "Oh, that is the custom in Russia. The wedding takes place normally on a Saturday or a Sunday. Irrespective of the season, after signing the register at the marriage office, married couples must visit the important national monuments near by. Regardless of his position, he must wear his service uniform for the wedding." The main idea behind all this was to rise above personal pleasure and remember their national duty to the freedom fighters. The custom was set to save national time, money and energy.

Amma, What is Your Duty is an illustration of a saying "child is the father of a man". Sudha Murty's daughter had taken up a voluntary charity assignment of teaching blind children in school. One day she came across a bright and ambitious boy who wanted to join St. Stephen's College, Delhi for further education but he had no money. Akshata saved the money she would have squandered on her birthday and handed it over to the boy. Mother Sudha Murty was impressed by daughter's gesture and started giving donations for the education of the deprived children.

Story of Two Doctors demonstrates the spirit of sacrifice in doctors for the welfare of the people. A doctor invented an injection for local anesthesia that can be used during operation. Nobody wanted to be a guinea pig. At last inventor doctor tested it on his own son. He took up a surgery on the sixth finger of his son before the members of Academy of Medical Sciences, so that the academy can approve the injection for public use. Unfortunately for the son, father had forgotten to mix one of the ingredients in the injection. The son was undergoing terrible agony during the operation but did not show it on his face. The medicine was approved. The story shows the selfless sacrifice of the entire family to further the cause of humanity.

A Journey through the Desert shows the inspiring effect of stories on the sensitive minds. Ram and Gopal were orphans living with their cruel uncle in a slum. Sudha Murty used to tell them stories in the garage while they repaired her car. Ram followed the moral of her stories in spirit; Gopal did not. The two labored hard during the day time. Ram joined a night school, completed a diploma in mechanical engineering. He established a state of the art service centre within ten years. He became an entrepreneur. Gopal did not utilize his time fruitfully. Gopal killed his time in day dreaming. As a result, he remained a garage boy throughout his life.

Dead Man's Riddle shows the value of elderly advice in life. A rich man died. He left seventeen horses, kilos of gold and tons of silver behind him. His will mentioned that the elder son should be given half of the total number of horses to the first son, two third of the remaining horses be given to the second son and the third son should get the two third horses of the remaining horses. Sons were unable to solve the riddle. An old friend of the diseased man who knew his friend's mind well, added his own horse, gave nine horses to the elder, six to the second and two to the third. The story brings out the importance of an elderly person in family. Murty summarized the moral of the story thus, "Experience is the best teacher in life. Elders have seen many ups and downs in their lives and interacted with many people. During the process they have acquired knowledge which cannot be taught in school or college."

I Will Do It narrates the noticeable incident from Narayan Murthy's childhood. Though Narayan Murthy qualified IIT entrance examination, middle class poverty prevented him from joining the Indian Institute of Technology. It did not discourage him thoroughly. He ardently followed the preaching of *Bhagawad Geeta* which said, "Your best friend is yourself and your worst enemy is yourself". While his friends worked in other offices, Narayan Murthy started his own IT company Infosys and employed thousands of IITians in it.

The Rainy Day is a metaphor for needy day. Sudha Murty's mother had advised her always to save some money from her routine income for emergency needs. Sudha Murty was working in TELCO and her husband Narayan Murthy was working in PCS after their marriage. Suddenly Narayan

Murthy decided to start a software company in collaboration with six of his colleagues. He needed seed capital. Sudha Murty had saved ten thousand rupees from her salary for a rainy day, which she was able to hand over to her husband. Story shows the importance of advice in life. Her mother had advised her to save some money and use it in extremely essential situation.

Doing What You Like is Freedom is a story of two different individuals. Punit was not allowed to do anything by his CA father. He was pampered to the core and needed his parents for everything. Sharad on the other hand was completely independent. He learned what he wanted to. He went to the places he fancied. Punit looked like a puppet whose reins were operated by his parents. Sharad looked a lively boy full of enthusiasm. Sudha Murty opined that children should be left to themselves, without external interference.

Gawramma's Letter conveys the role that a story and storyteller play on sensitive minds. Sudha Murty addressed a group of college students. A girl asked her a question as to how she faced difficult problems in life. Sudha Murty narrated a story of Hanuman from *Ramayana* who lifted the entire Dronagiri Mountain when he was in a state of confusion. It had a moral that, "When you come across difficulties, you have to grow bigger than the problem." Elderly lady

Gawramma had narrated this story to her when she was a child. Stories from Indian mythology have shaped the character of many Indians from generation to generation.

Who Is Great narrates the importance of viewing the action from different angles. Teacher asked her student in the class to deck herself with lot of gold and visit her house in the moonless night. The girl obeyed her and walked with a lot of gold on her person. She was interrupted by a thief on the way. She promised the thief that she would give it on her way back. The thief let her go to her teacher. He did not take the gold when she offered it to him during her return. Students interpreted the story differently. Sudha Murty told them that the person should be assessed from various angles. Only then the right image of the person emerges.

A for Honesty explains the role of honesty in shaping the character of a student. Murty's son was studying in a college in the US. He once misread a digital figure in examination and calculated the sum accordingly. When the results came, he was given 'A' grade for that examination. Boy thought that his teacher had made a mistake in assessment. He asked his teacher about it. But the teacher was right. He had assessed not only his answer sheet but also his student"s entire personality during the academic year.

A Lesson in Ingratitude narrates the story of ungratefulness of Suresh. The school and the college where he went helped him complete his education in all respects. Professor Rao fed him for five years. The librarian provided him residence and clothes. Suresh accumulated tremendous wealth in the latter part of his life. He had a palatial bungalow, a farm house, silver wares, dozens of servants. In spite of all these riches, he never visited the teachers who had done so much for him. He was arrogant enough to say, "I feel everyone in college helped me because they wanted to feel better about themselves. After all, I was a very good student. I am convinced that people help others only with a selfish motive."

My Biggest Mistake conveys the way in which the boss should conduct the office. Sudha Murty prepared a social welfare programme after seven days of hard work. Her student Nalini deleted the programme by mistake before it was properly saved. She began to repent and cry. Sudha Murty sympathetically forgave her. She said, "That incident taught me that when you become a leader you should be kind and forgiving to your subordinates. It is not fear that binds you to your boss. Affection, openness and the appreciation of your qualities builds a long lasting relationship."

The Secret reveals the principle that gender discrimination is wrong. Boy and girl both possess similar qualities, emotions, attitudes and habits. Besides the natural differences, girl does not essentially differ from boy and vice versa. Sudha Murty sends a clear message that a person gets known by the qualities he or she possesses, not by the gender.

Summing Up

To conclude, it may be surmised that in contemporary English literature, non-fictional works and language has its own impact on the world literature in English. Sudha Murty's contribution in this field is immense. The present paper deals about the real situation in India, especially the marriage system, child marriage (*Bal-Vivaha*), and women's education. The spiritual meaning of education is derived and self-realization of the real religious philosophy is conveyed with the special references of the fictional book *How I Taught My Grandmother to Read and Other Stories*. The real prayer to God and real pooja of the God is not to visit any pilgrimage but to help needy people and self-realization. "To help the poor is Godliness."

The literary contribution of Sudha Murty in the contemporary English literature is a milestone for the readers of literature. Sudha Murty has observed the society minutely and with the help of her own experiences, she has prorated the beautiful ladies characters. The protagonists of the stories are representatives of all the Indian ladies who are suffering from educational, social, financial, and domestic problems. The old lady Krishtakka's isolation is the live picture of the real education and the spirit of education. In nutshell, in the contemporary Indian English literature, the literary contribution of Sudha Murthy is probably dealing with feminist problems that are educational, social, domestic, cultural etc in the post-modernism.

Reference

Murty, Sudha (2004), *How I Taught My Grandmother to Read and Other Stories,* Penguin Book India

5

Three Thousand Stitches:

Ordinary People, Extraordinary Lives

"Coming from a middle-class background of Northern Karnataka, where good education was the only insurance policy, I started reading and writing very early." – Sudha Murty

As is observed from various writings, Sudha Murty explores many personal experiences in her non-fiction title *Three Thousand Stitches*. A quick read, the book is full of important life lessons and values that readers can take away and apply to their own lives.

Notably a powerful signature in India known for her hard work and dedication and her concern for the social reforms, Sudha Murty's social reforms includes almost all the fields i.e. health care, emancipation of women, public hygiene, poverty, art and culture, rural development in association with Karnatak Government etc. She has significantly contributed to the literature of Kannada and English. Her struggles are obvious and noted by people who know her, and all the stories have an honest confession of her thoughts and their transformation into a positive outcome.

Three Thousand Stitches is a collection of eleven different stories, which Sudha draws from her personal life, with a message engraved in every story. The main story revolves around the lives of the sex workers or *devadasis*, her determination to make them self-sustainable, and to get rid of the label of dishonor that was attached to them.

Three Thousand Stitches is the title story of this collection written by a social worker for the betterment of the neglected women of *devadasi* culture. *Devdasi* culture existed for some time in the 7th century during the reigns of Cholas and Pandyas. During that period, it was not looked down upon, but in modern days it is akin to prostitution. The so called *devdasis* were ignorant of their future, they were ostracized by the society, and they suffered. Their ignorant, but firm belief that Goddess will protect them became true when Sudha Murty entered into their life and thought of their reformation. She was Goddess for the *devdasis* but in reality Sudha was a woman who struggled hard to make them realize their value as a human being. Initially *devdasis* rejected her, they didn't listen to her as, "—they all suffered at the hands of a society that exploited them and filled them with guilt and shame as a final insult."

Later she changed her appearance. "I wore a two-hundred-rupee sari, a big *bindi*, a *mangalsutra* and glass bangles. I transformed myself into the '*bharatiya nari*', the stereotypical, traditional Indian woman, and took my father along with me to meet the *devadasis*." (p. 13) It was then they accepted her, listened to her and followed her. An autobiographical note written in First person narration is so powerful that it wrenches your heart. In this story, the helplessness of the author is beautifully narrated when the *devdasis* rejected her presence. Her struggles to make them accept her, ultimately her victory, with an old *devdasi's* oration and the precious gift they gave to her is amazingly depicted in words. This experience has definitely shown the path to many people around who can't raise a huge empire of refuge for sufferers but at least can lend a helping hand. The title of the story is justified in last few lines by an old *devdasi*, "We want to give our *akka* a special gift."

This is a linear presentation with a single theme of reformation of neglected class, efforts made by a single woman who has lost the battle initially, but later becomes a winner with the support of her father and her co-worker Abhay. Her makeover also helped in her efforts. Indianess is emphasized by the use of Hindi and Kannada words "They called me *akka* or 'elder sister' in Kannada. The *'bharatiya nari', 'Namaskaram, Amma, Kalash, bhandara 'man— bahujanhitaya, bahujansukhaya*—it must provide compassionate aid regardless of caste, creed, language or religion. (p. 8), as if she wants to make it and be sure that she is Indian irrespective of the English language, she has chosen for narrating her success of reforming *devdasis*.

It is reported that because of her efforts, today there are no temple prostitutes left in the State of Karnataka. The book also discloses her other personal experiences, like being called 'cattle class' because of her language and dressing, and to be the only woman to study engineering in an all men's college. She describes her journey from being a little girl to grandmother, from being ignorant to becoming an inspiration, her struggles and victories and offerind advice, sometimes boldly and sometimes softly.

As already stated, the first story, from which the book gets its title, is the most touching story for me. It is about her earliest days of building the Infosys Foundation. The book talks about a lot of social issues and problems like *devadasi,* addictions and slave trading. But they do not talk about how to sympathize with a victim of such problems, how to empathize with the situation and the people involved. It also strengthened my belief in the quote, "Where there's a will, there's a way." If you really feel that you need to do something, to find and create your own identity, you will definitely find the guiding light of your life. There are a few very innocent anecdotes, talking about her grandparents, about her love for food and Bollywood and one story about her dad's act of kindness, which makes you feel warm in the heart and gives you deep satisfaction. You may not share the same belief or faith with someone you deeply love or admire, but the fact is that both of you are humans and both have your right to your own opinions. Something similar happen with the author when she visited Kashi, a place her grandmother wished to visit at least once in her life. Unfortunately, she couldn't, and the author lives through her late granny's memories in the polluted waters of the Ganga.

Three Thousand Stitches introduces us to the *devadasi* community and their sordid lives. Sudha Murty is a key contributor in making their lives better through her determination and her father's important advice.

In *How To Beat The Boys*, a seventeen-year-old Sudha strives to become an engineer despite all the obstacles that come her way. Sudha goes on to become the only female student in her entire college, showing her strength and perseverance. *How to beat Boys* deals with the theme of feminism, rather re-enforced experience that says nothing is impossible, for any woman can beat the boys. Emphasis is laid on women's education with the message when she can do it, why not others to make a community of successful women. She doesn't hesitate, instead is confident and proud for being a student of enginering. "I'm talking about the Basappa Veerappa Bhoomaraddi College of Engineering and Technology in Hubli, a medium-sized town in the State of Karnataka in India." Murty, Sudha. *Three Thousand Stitches*." (p. 20). A touch of humour or rather a proud humour by giving details of importance of studying at a small place engineering college and emphasizing the importance of family being a core of 'Indian culture' is the highlight.

In chapter three, *Food For Thought*, you will learn about the diverse vegetables and fruits used in Indian cooking and their surprising places of origin. *Food for Thought* is an interesting experience of the author that gives an insight into mystical importance of nature with the religions and culture, mythology, *trishanku* state of man and myths associated with it. Vishwamitra created a new world for *Trishanku* and called it *Trishanku Swarga*. He even created vegetables that belonged neither to the earth nor heaven. (p. 36). Story of the origin of banana fruit and the power of a sage to create a fruit and the myths related to it is mentioned through the story of sage Durvsa, "farm—one was a chilli called Gandhar or Ravana chilli"(pp. 35-36) Importance of modern technology is also narrated as well "Today, Google is like my grandmother. I log on to the website any time I require an explanation of something I don't understand or want to learn about."

Discussing dishes from Mysore State also mention the etymology of the dessert Gulab Jamun, in Moghals reign Kashmiri Kheer, discussion on dishes of Maharashtra. Her visit to her friends house gathering interesting information gives the impression of National Integration. It's simply an informative experience with no particular theme to emphasize.

In *Three Handfuls of Water*, Sudha Murty is introduced to a holy place--Kashi--by her grandparents. She learns the significance of going there and ends up taking a vow that opens to her the door to freedom. *Three Hand Fulls of Water* shows the importance of Hindu rituals that cannot be ruled out, a story narrating the importance of Kashi and river Ganges with author's experiences and her conversations with her grandmother and the way she taught her the importance of these religious places."Kashi is one of the most sacred places on earth. The river Ganga flows there. It is believed that Lord Vishwanath, the Lord of the universe, resides there and gives boons to everyone. (p. 43)." Kashi is protected by Bhairavnath, who is a great and loyal servant of Lord Shiva. If you go to Kashi and don't see the Kaal Bhairav temple, your *yatra* or journey is considered incomplete. (p. 43-44)." Beliefs associated with all these find a mention here.

In the fifth chapter, *Cattle Class*, she recounts an incident that took place at an international airport. Also published on various media channels, this story elicits a thought-provoking message about the society that readily judges people by their appearance. *Cattle Class* is an experience that deals with moral and social conduct. A small incident about how appearances can be deceptive. And about arrogance too. One shouldn't judge people on the grounds of money and pompous appearance; people may have a grounded personality and they do not want to show off their wealth. Moral of the story - a lesson for the so called sophisticated class that money is not everything.

A Life Unwritten is the story of the writer's father, a doctor, who is temporarily posted in a remote village. While there, he delivers a baby of an unmarried girl and ends up doing something kind that makes a difference in her life forever. *A Life Unwritten* is a heartfelt experience of Murty's father performing his duties as a doctor with a generous heart. It is about a woman's struggle and how a kind hearted Mentor can change one's life. A woman who wanted to die as she has suffered in the hands of a man and so her daughter will also have to suffer 'Oh my God! It's a girl!' she cried. 'Her life will be just like mine—under the cruel pressure of the men in the family. And she doesn't even have a father!'(p. 62). Fate of a woman and here a Doctor's help became life changer. The story also throws light on Sudha Murty's moral education along with academics, to fight back till one becomes a winner. She too became a mentor and helped many people, particularly women

This seventh story titled *No Place like Home* depicts people who worked as housemaids in the Middle East and their horrific experiences. *No Place Like Home* is author's kind heartedness and sacrifice, Murty meets some women who have been taken to Middle East to work as maids. And their tortures and helplessness has touched her so much that without wasting time she arranged one way fare for these tortured women to bring them back to India, keeping aside construction of her new office.

A Powerful Ambassador is about Sudha Murty`s interest in films and her keen and observing nature has perhaps taught her and given her a training to become a writer of class. Extensive traveling all over the world helped her to know the various cultures as well as importance of Bollywood everywhere and its deep rooted impact. She herself accepts, "Necessary prerequisites consist of a tight story, good music, crisp conversation, excellent script and dialogues, fine acting by the lead roles, appropriate costumes, outstanding direction and careful editing." "My deep interest in films took me to the next level—assessing the acting abilities of the heroes and the skills of the director." (p. 84).

Interestingly in *A Powerful Ambassador,* Murty explains how movies were considered a luxury in her village, Shiggaon. During her college days, she was an avid moviegoer, often visiting the movie theatre with her friends to watch classic Bollywood movies. Further, when she tours the world, she is thrilled to learn that the charm of Bollywood films and their actors has not only captured Indians, but people worldwide.

Rasleela and the Swimming Pool, the ninth story in the collection, tells Draupadi and Krishna's story from both the writer's and her grandchildren's perspectives. In this story a helpless Grandmother narrates two stories of Indian mythology to her grandchildren. She told those stories to them which her grandmother had narrated to her, "I thought that they would visualize the scenes just like I had."(p. 94), 'the same tale of Lord Krishna and the *gopikas*. Since I had their attention, I added the story of Akshaya Patra too.(p. 94). Retelling of the stories by the two grandchildren was about a whole westernized version that astounded the author, and helped her realize that now it was impossible for her to explain to them the importance of Indian mythology and the moral lessons that they impart.

A Day in Infosys Foundation gives the picture of author's busy schedule where she cannot have her social life, cannot justify her social commitments in the family. She invites her childhood friend Shobhato to spend some time, but her friend leaves the office as Murty has to do some more work in the office. Her friend asks her, "Tell me, why do you continue to give your remaining years to this thankless job?

You can sit back, relax, spend time with your grandchildren," (p. 112). Her friend's suggestion is rejected then and there, "The truth is that I am the luckiest of them all. I love what I do and…" (p.113). When an old friend criticizes Sudha Murty for not sparing an hour for her, she is invited to spend a day with her at Infosys Foundation. Seeing her work, the friend becomes aware of the huge responsibility Sudha Murty has. To Mrs. Murty, her day is nothing short of a marathon. This is the theme of the tenth chapter, *A day in Infosys Foundation.*

Now we come to chapter eleven, *I Can't, We Can: A Detailed Sum.*

When Sudha Murty first discovered the term AA i.e. Alcoholic Anonymous, she grew curious. Multiple questions arose in her mind: What is AA and how it plays a role in an alcoholic's life? Is alcoholism hereditary? What is the success rate of de-addiction? and so on.

Researching about it on the internet was not enough. She wanted to gather the information first-hand. A friend's relative, also a chairman of an AA committee, opens a pool of information to her by inviting her to an open meeting in a church.

There, participants share how alcohol brought them to the lowest points in their lives and how AA helped them cope with them. Several of them were now dedicated to educating others about it.

It takes years for people to become sober. However, it isn't guaranteed. There are cases of relapses as well. Because of this, they meet regularly to control their urges.

AA is active in 186 countries and has helped many alcoholics become sober.

After leaving that meeting, Murty remembers the famous Marathi play *Ekach Pyala,* where the first peg of alcohol ruins a married couple's life.

Alcoholism is a medically recognized disease.

Alcoholics Anonymous deals primarily with alcohol, though some people fall for smoking and drugs as well. Nobody can predict who will develop an addiction. But, organizations like AA contribute to a better society and give people hope.

I Can't, We Can In a family wedding, the author's cousin wanted to introduce her to her friend's daughter, Murty interrupts but,'My friend's daughter is a bright student and . . .' 'Is she planning to apply for a job at Infosys?' I interrupted her. 'Because I really can't . . .'(p. 115) This needs to be mentioned because the word in title used is 'I can't,' which is later converted into 'We Can' when she visits AA organization, and then when the girl said,'Ma'am, my father was an alcoholic.' (p. 116). Social reformer herself Murty came to know about the organizations of Alcoholic Alcohol. She attended their meetings and was impressed by their determination. Though this story directly has nothing to do in this brief autobiography of hers but definitely her appreciation for other such organization meant a lot for people who are struggling hard to come out the devil's grip. Sudha Murty in this brief autobiography is concerned only with those incidents and experiences in her life that has helped her to develop her personality, and a thought process. A strategy was made long before in her mind and implemented later in life. What makes Sudha Murty different from the other contemporary women writers is that she's basically an engineer, an Information Technology professional. So therein lies the difference of mindset. Her language is simple first-hand experience with no ornaments used; purpose is to be understood by the masses.

The stories Sudha Murty writes, whether fiction or non-fiction, are light to read but have a lot of value. Her books do not contain fancy wordplay or extravagant sentences. Some of them even seem like a blank stating of events, but what I get to learn from her writing is still worth it for me. I think she is very open-minded w.r.t her generation and she feels like a person loyal to her roots.

Summing Up

In a nutshell, Sudha Murty's dedication in *How to Beat the Boys* is inspirational because she broke stereotypes and followed her dream to become an engineer with flying results.

Three Thousand Stitches is a collection of 11 short stories that draw from her real life experiences, as an individual and as the chairperson of Infosys Foundation, which does considerable work for the underprivileged.

The stories can be clearly divided into two sections - personal and philanthropic. And what's interesting is how often her personal interactions and chance encounters lead to identifying "problem" areas, which can be addressed through the aegis of Infosys Foundation.

Whether it is helping poor, abused women stranded in the UAE (*No Place Like Home*) or alcoholism (*I Can't, We Can*), it is Murty's openness to listen to people that changes lives - and grabs the reader's attention. Simply told, some of the tales in themselves are quite moving.

Murty's style of writing is completely without frills. And as a reader, that's disappointing. She narrates the stories or dialogues as they happened in real life, but the language fails to add any depth or emotion. So after a point, you are left plodding through the book. Also, never for a moment could I shrug off the feeling that the purpose of the stories is to instruct. A dash of humour and, if I may dare to say so, a hint of wickedness would have done wonders to the book. I mean, one respects but can barely relate to someone who has, at her worst, lied at home to watch movies.

Three Thousand Stitches however, is worth a read because of the real stories and the real people at its heart. Fact, as they say, is often more interesting than fiction.

References

Ghosh, Suktara (2017-08-18), "'Three Thousand Stitches': Sudha Murty Roots Her Book in Reality", The Quint.

"Three Thousand Stitches". Penguin Random House India. Retrieved 2021-11-15.

"Book review: Sudha Murthy's Three Thousand Stitches isn't a book you'll remember". Hindustan Times, 2017-10-20.

Murty, Sudha. Three Thousand Stitches, Random House Publishers India Pvt. Ltd. Kindle Edition.

6

The Sage with Two Horns &

The Gopi Diaries

"Vision without action is merely a dream; action without vision is merely passing time; but vision and action together can change the world. *"- Sudha Murty*

Here in this chapter we will introduce you to two books by Sudha Murty—*The Sage with Two Horns* and *Gopi Diaries*.

The Sage with Two Horns

From quarrels among gods and the follies of great sages to the benevolence of kings and the virtues of ordinary mortals, India's favorite author Sudha Murty spins fresh accounts of lesser-known stories from Indian mythology. Accompanied by delightful illustrations and narrated in an unassuming fashion, *The Sage with Two horns* is sure to delight fans of Sudha Murty.

This is the fifth and last book of her *Unusual Tales from Mythology* series featuring kings and queens, gods and goddesses, sages and extraordinary men and women of wisdom. It is the follow-up to *The Man from the Egg, Serpent's Revenge, The Upside-Down King* and *The Daughter from the Wishing Tree*.

Over the five volumes, Murty has gone through different versions of the *Ramayana*, the *Mahabharata* and the *Bhagvad Gita* in different States and languages.

The book has four sections. The first one *Guruve Namaha* narrates stories about the relationship between *Guru* and *Shishya*. In the next section Kings who became saints tells stories where the rulers of land leave their throne to become Sages. The next section Raja Prithvi Pathi is all about Great and Just Kings. And the fourth section A Bag of surprises literally has a wide variety of surprising stories. The last section Tales from Vault has some folk stories.

There are a few stories that used to be popular a decade ago but not so much in recent times, so it's a delight to read these stories again. My favorite stories are *A Pigeon's Weight - Story of Shibi Charkravarthi, The Girl Who Wanted Death Penalty* - the story of a king named Punyanidhi, *The Mistery of Identical Nose Ring* - Story of Purandaradasaru.

"They may seem to differ in many ways, but the thread remains the same in all versions. Some supporting characters mentioned in mythology have their own stories to tell with their own perspectives of life," she says. *The Sage with Two Horns* has stories ranging from quarrels among gods and the follies of great sages to the benevolence of kings and the virtues of ordinary mortals.

Each book is independent of the other but even together, they are far from being exhaustive, she writes. Published by Puffin, the book has illustrations by Priyankar Gupta.

Murty says there is a powerful force in the universe that can be called by any name. "This force is an eternal witness of our deeds, both good and bad, and is always there to guide us if we pay attention to it and listen to it carefully," she says.

Murty has written novels, technical books, travelogues, collections of short stories and non-fiction pieces, and bestselling books for children.

According to Sohini Mitra, associate publisher at Penguin Random House India, there could be no better way to celebrate and soak in the festive spirit than experiencing the joy of a well-told story by the ever-favourite Sudha Murty.

Now we turn to *The Gopi Diaries.*

The Gopi Diaries

It is significant to note first that *The Gopi Diaries* is a series of three books for children about a dog called Gopi. Told in Gopi's voice, the first book, *Coming Home*, begins with Gopi going to his new home, and tells the story of how he settles down with his loving, human family. How Gopi sees the world around him and what he thinks of the people in his life give the story a truly unique flavour. Written in Sudha Murty's inimitable style, these are books children and adults will treasure as the simple stories talk of basic values even when told from a dog's perspective.

Book two takes the story ahead after a year, while book three will be out soon. The story is narrated from Gopi's point of view which makes it all the more adorable. In *Finding Love*, Gopi has now grown up from a young pup to an adult dog. He narrates how he loves spending time with his favourite humans, the mischiefs he does, and how content his life is.

Gopi's tales are inspired by Sudha Murty's pet dog named Gopi. It is noted that some of the characters in the stories are based on real-life people, including the author and her husband, Infosys Chairman N.R. Narayana Murthy, which makes these stories all the more familiar and relatable. The book is written in simple and concise language, which makes it perfect for young readers who have started reading on their own. The beautiful illustrations by Sandhya Prabhat make the book an enjoyable read. This is an endearing tale of Gopi, the beloved pet dog.

Excerpts from an interview#

"Initially, I thought I wouldn't be able to write anything except that Gopi is a handsome golden retriever. Then, I saw the world through him. It would have been very different to be brought to a new family, be taught different things, and assimilate into the family," she says.

The objective of the book is to inculcate a love for animals among children along with spotlighting the values of sharing, caring, and compassion. As a child, Sudha had a dog called Raja, who passed away. Though it is sad that a dog leaves you sooner than you think, she believes that the love stays on. That love can be transferred to another pet without diluting what you had for the first one, she feels.

"With animals, you don't require a language to communicate. It also makes you careful about how you treat them. Kids are at an impressionable age where they understand these things. When it rains, the first thing you will think about is the safety of your pet. In winter, I wrap Gopi in a rug because I know he feels cold," she says. Gopi is not alone; he has company in the form of two other dogs, one two-legged and the other three-legged, strays adopted from the shelter. "There are so many dogs out there, on the streets and in shelters. If a colony can adopt three-four dogs, vaccinate them, and treat them with love and affection, children will also learn to be compassionate." She says that taking care of a pet is also a fun activity, and a good opportunity for children to enjoy the outdoors by taking their pets out on walks. "They learn to socialise with other people and listen to different sounds." Almost everything that's in *The Gopi Diaries* is from real life.

In it, Sudha mentions a comical moment when Gopi pulls Ajji's *dupatta*. "Today, if I had worn a salwar-kameez instead of a sari, he would have pulled off the *dupatta*," she says with a laugh. Today, Gopi is content playing with a soft toy Sudha has bought him to celebrate the launch of his book. Tired of playing all day, he goes to sleep, at Sudha's feet, as she watches adoringly. She speaks of a visit to a school in Bengaluru to introduce the book. "When I spoke about Gopi, they were all excited. They had brought their soft toy dogs along and refused to part with them when I asked," she chuckles, adding, "I think as four-year-olds, it was the right age for them to grasp the importance of having a pet and caring for it."

Gopi is a small pup who loves his mother and siblings; but he was taken away from them. Gopi then tells us how he felt after he was brought to his Ajji's house by his Appa. He was happy getting a new and caring family. Gopi talking about the environment in the house, the schedule and behaviour of each family member made me think if pets really think that way? (Cute! If they do.) The interaction between Gopi and his Ajja was the funniest of all. Every time Gopi tried persuading Ajja to play and got rejected is hilarious. Deep inside Ajja cared deeply for Gopi.

A book written for children can also engage the adults. Not just children but every single person can start reading this book and get hooked until we realize that we are already at the last page. It barely takes an hour to read. But that hour is full of cuteness, kindness, zeal, smiles and laughter. Takes us away from the distractions of the world.

Remarkably this beautiful book tells the story of Gopi, a golden retriever who is adopted by the author and her family. The book is narrated from his point of view, right from the time when he is born and sees little white fur balls around him, to the time when he is adopted by a young and handsome man who turns out to be Rohan Murthy, Sudha and Narayan Murthy's son. Gopi the pup is taken to Rohan's home where he is baffled by the sight of two grey-haired old ladies who hold a plate with flames on it and move it round and round in front of him! What on earth could that be? As readers, we know what this is but Gopi is perplexed and is a little scared of the fire!

Gopi then adjusts to his new home. He discovers that Rohan is his 'appa,' and he meets his Ajja (Narayan Murthy) and Ajji (Sudha Murty.) Narayan Murthy, the famous IT industrialist, makes an appearance as himself, as do other members of the Murty family- - Rohan Murthy, and Akshata Murty's daughters, Krishna and Anoushka Sunak. Narayan Murthy or ajja as he is called doesn't like dogs but does he warm up to Gopi? You have to find out! The adventures of Gopi are delightful -- we love the chapter when he goes to the vet and he imagines what the other dogs tell him about the vet!

Sandhya Prabhat's illustrations bring out the essence of Gopi's relationships with his people and how he views those around him. In some ways, that's how children view the world around them too -- magnified, exhilarating and intense!

Written in Sudha Murty's beautiful and lucid style, this book about animals will warm your heart the way *Black Beauty* or books by Gerald Durrell warmed our hearts as children. This is the perfect Indian animal book to grow up with, and we love that it is going to be series! The highlight of the book is the author's ability to get inside

Gopi's head and how he sees everything differently. The book is a great way to get children to see the world from a dog's perspective and to understand kindness, gentleness, and empathy. The book is filled with exciting incidents and has many vibrant characters - Sudha Murty's family as well as the people who work for her and even this book's editor!

References

Murty, Sudha (2021), The Sage with Two Horns, Penguin Random Hose India.

Murty, Sudha (2020) The Gopi Diaries: Finding Love,

Murty, Sudha (2019), The Gopi Diaries: Coming Home,HarperCollins Publishers India

7

Gently Falls the Bakula &

House of Cards

The 'Universal Force' is an eternal witness of our deeds, both good and bad, and is always there to guide us if we pay attention to it and listen to it carefully."- Sudha Murty

Feminism can be defined as a conscious attempt towards revaluing women's experience, rethinking the canons of text, revising the recognition of socio cultural, discourse and language, economic and political conditions in the society representing biological differences and their implications. Recent gyro texts express female creativity encompassing various styles, themes, genres and structures.

Sudha Murty as a feminist opposes the customs, norms and traditions of a society which tends to place a woman in a position inferior to that of a man, socially, politically, physically and economically. She has taken up themes of rebellion against the existing social setup through her women characters. Her women are no longer weak, meek and submissive creatures, instead they realize that they have roles to play in a family and in a society like their male counterparts. The women in her novels have preferences, prejudices and raise their voices to be heard. They emphasize their individuality and emerge as new women awakened to face the challenges and lead a meaningful and dignified life, irrespective of the insensible social criticism.

Gently Falls The Bakula

Gently falls the Bakula was Sudha Murty's first novel written three decades ago in Kannada, and translated into English recently. The book records in a sensitive way, how marriages disintegrate as ambition and self-interest take their toll. The novel remains remarkably relevant in its analysis of modern values and work ethics. Manu, the first law giver in our Hindu tradition, himself has assigned a high status and dignity to woman. His dictum is an evidence of this: *"Yatranaryastupujyante, ramante tatradevata"* (III,56), which says, "God exists where women are respected" but very few women in our state exercise their freedom; most of them are either oppressed or neglected to a secondary position. Determined to rebuild her life against all odds, she becomes a revolutionary woman. This one is a well-written story about how two people, equal yet from different backgrounds, fall in love with each other. But, then sets in the old stereotypes of male dominance and ignorant attitude toward females.

Gently falls the Bakula is a beautiful story of two different individuals-- Srikant and Shrimati Deshpande, both approach life very differently from each other. Srikant is a very ambitious guy from the very beginning who falls in love with the very intelligent yet simple girl Shrimati for whom nothing is more important than Srikant's companionship and his happiness. This simple story turns into a complex one, when Srikant starts loving his career more than Shrimati and when she starts realizing that her life is going nowhere apart from revolving around her husband and his needs.

Though here we sympathize with Shrimati a lot than Srikant, I felt somewhere she is also responsible for his change in behaviour. I felt she was too submissive than needed. Submissive to some extent is fine in any relationship but if it goes beyond necessary then obviously that person is taken for granted and that's what happened here too. The open ending is quite appropriate here, but still, I would like to assume that at one point in time they again met and lived with each other happily.

Initially the story opens with the background of a school where Shrikant and Shrimati study. Both were neighbours, equally talented and intelligent while Shrimati is a little bit more brilliant than Shrikant. Shrimati took History and Shrikant got admission in IIT Bombay. Soon they realized the relation was more than friendship. She was very special to him. They met under the old bakula tree and there was always a string of bakula flowers on her hair. The smell of the flower is so nostalgic to Shrikant that throughout the story bakula plays a very important role. Shrikant marries Shrimati without the permission of their families and shift to Bombay, a mechanical city with no human relationships. His people were greedy and they wanted a bride who was richer and younger than Shrimati. The wedding ceremony was simple but Shrimati was contented. Just like a typical Indian bride, Shrimati wanted to win over her mother-in-law. So she helped her in the kitchen. But Gangakka didn't want Shrimati to enter into it.(page 70)

At first they lived in a small single bedroom apartment at Bandra. Shrikant was hard working; sometimes he would work even at night. Gradually she became one among the people in the crowded trains. Shrimati got a small job to pay money for her mother- in-law for the loan that was taken for Shrikant's study. After sixteen months she resigned from her job. Shrikant became the manager and she explains the story of Bhamati to her husband. Bhamati signifies all those women who sacrifice their youth for the betterment of their husbands. Shrimati wanted to enroll for her Ph.D but he was shifted to Delhi. Many unexpected things happen in life and Shrikant 's boss was extremely happy with his performance in Delhi and he was promoted as a project manager and sent to Los Angels, USA. They shifted to America and life was totally changed. She had been in touch with Professor Kollins. In USA, she was fascinated by the market, the roads, the people and everything. Soon he became the General Manager and came back to India, life was at its peak, a new car and driver, three bed room flat facing the sea at Bandra. Shrimati was amazed, for everything was beyond her imagination. Shrikant had become extremely busy and was touring a lot. He travelled twenty to twenty – five days a month. His life revolved around his company, nothing else.

A story told in a simple style. It questions the choices women make and are they happy with those choices. Are they happy with the sacrifices they make for their partner to succeed and I feel this happens in every culture. For any one person to be insanely successful, somebody close to that person pays the price.

The bakula flowers are the attachments to her love letters, which carry the symbolic meaning that the fragrance and beauty of their love will never fade to shadows. It also sheds light on how Shrimati, being the woman, made the sacrifice of ignoring her interests for Shrikant, the male protagonist she falls in love with. She lays aside her aspirations and academic talents staying at home, while

Shrikant focuses on his career entirely; not acknowledging any situations on Shrimati's part. Finally, Shrimati takes the brave soul choice in departing to the US and pursuing her dream of getting a PhD.

The end is when Shrikant realises his cruelty in not giving Shrimati her due, and regretting his decision in being totally aloof and busy with his domineering self. But by then it was too late. The bakula tree that had separated their houses and whose blossoming, exquisite flowers that exemplified the love they had, had fallen.

Shrimati and Shrikant are two intelligent competitive classmates. They hail from a small town in Karnataka,are neighbours and their families are involved in an ancient feud. Shrimati is very intelligent and could ace anything she put her mind to, but she loved history and studied for the love of the subject. Shrikant wanted to be an acheiver. Both follow their dreams and fall in love and get married. But with success comes a high price. The couple slowly start drifting apart. Shrikant's meteoric rise to the top makes him ambivalent towards his wife. He wants to acheive more and more and treats Shrimati like his secretary who is there to do everything to run his life smoothly. Being childless too makes Shrimati more lonely, adoption is not an option as Shrikant does not support the notion.

Though the language is very simple which Sudha Murthy has used, yet I think that brings a lot more beauty to this story. The connection with the story for me started instantly from the very first page as the background and religious practices which Sudha Murthy has explained here, are so real.

Overall, a good yet critical read, thoroughly enjoyed. For its simple writing and good content, every Indian woman will feel connected to the story in one or the other way. This book taught us how a very obvious matter goes unseen, how feelings fade and how unknowingly we hurt people. It rightly brings out the fact that it is us who fail, and not the relationships

Feminism in Context

It is apt to mention here that feminist literary criticism has established itself as a foundational notion in literature. To some extent, the feminism of the 1960s has influenced modern feminist literary critique. There is feminism in the classical and traditional writings even prior to the women's movement. In their publications, they strove to find answers to the issue of women's inequality. This list includes works by Virginia Woolf, Jane Austen, and John Stuart Mill, all of whom are known for their feminist perspectives. In the 1960s, the women's movement was primarily a literary one. It recognised the importance of literature's portrayal of women, and saw it as necessary to challenge and question the male dominated society and to reclaim power and respect.

Primarily the function of theory and the nature of language have been the subject of many debates.

Simultaneously the nature of language has long been the subject of discussion. There was a debate on whether or not there is a distinct language for women. Language is gendered, according to Virginia Woolf in her essay *A Room of One's Own*. Women who begin novel writing are surprised to discover that there isn't a standard sentence available to them. Dale Spender argues that language is sexist because males have had the authority to define the meanings it contains, and these meanings represent men's perspective of reality rather than women's. Language has become a shared resource, according to their assessment. Most feminists, however, disdained the use of slovenly language and instead created their own clear and pure literary style.

Many feminists, both in theory and in practice, highlighted the importance of context-dependent language. When it came to writing, Jane Austen was the master of her craft.

The role of theory: This spawned three distinct feminisms. Some people prefer the English form, while others prefer the Anglo-American version. This kind of feminism is more cautious and suspicious. Traditional critical notions like subject, motif, and character are still very much a part of their work. And they see literature as a collection of portrayals of women's lives and experiences that may be compared to the facts of life. The second kind of feminist critique is that which originated in the United Kingdom. It's not like the US at all.

As a result, lumping it in with a 'nontheoretical category' is an evident mistake. 'It tends to be 'Socialist feminist,' in orientation associated with cultural materialism or Marxism.' French feminism, on the other hand, focuses more on theory than the other two. Post-structuralists like Lacan, Foucault, and Derrida provided the framework for their work. Indian feminists are influenced by the 1960s women's movement.

Sudha Murty is one of the few Indian feminists who is still active in the country today. Penguin has been her primary publisher for a number of her works. Her work has been translated in more than fifteen languages including Hindi, Marathi, Telugu etc. The themes of feminism are prevalent throughout Sudha Murty's works. Although she doesn't explicitly critique the male-dominated culture, the characters in her stories question it. Her protagonists are from middle-class families. They are obedient, clever, and selfless in their actions.

The Bold and Determined Female Characters

Synopsis of *Gently Falls the Bakula:* Shrimati and Shrikanth, the two main characters, play significant roles in this storey. Srikanth's neighbour, Shrimati, lives nearby. 'They went to the same high school in Hubli, a tiny town in North Karnataka.' They have a fierce rivalry. Shrimati is consistently recognised and rewarded by her educators. Friends and professors alike show their admiration for her. Even Shrikant is aware of how formidable a foe she is. In spite of this, he develops feelings for her and she reciprocates. They wed....... It is a little world she inhabits after marriage. She doesn't pay attention to the direction of her career. For the sake of her spouse, she gives up her time, education, and ability to make her own judgments. To her husband, she is nothing but a passive, obedient spectre. When her husband is out at work, she devotes herself to serving and awaiting his return. Shrikant, her spouse, on the other hand, works hard to improve his technical abilities and quickly rises through the ranks of the company. He sets up his own business. In the process, he neglects and forgets his wife's contribution to his progress.

This message was communicated symbolically by Sudha Murthy. Shrimati sacrifices her job for her husband, just as the Bakula flowers fill the air with their sweet scent. Shrikanth, a classmate of Shrimati's, proposes to her. She is a constant source of inspiration for him, never bringing attention to herself or her own issues. His mother and sister's bad conduct is known to him, but he chooses to remain quiet, allowing Shrimati to bear the brunt of it. They go out of their way to make fun of her and make her feel humiliated. Yet, Shrimati devotes her life to her husband. She's bright and smart, but she doesn't give a damn about her professional future. In spite of her loneliness, she hopes for Shrikant's success and quietly bears the weight of his accomplishments. He'll never be able to get to the top without her unwavering backing. Shrikant's ego, on the other hand, is adamant that she be excluded from the credit for his success because of her contribution.

Every time he looks back, he sees it as his accomplishment, not hers. He treats her almost like a personal assistant who takes care of all of his responsibilities. – Shrimati considers the accomplishments of her spouse to be her own. Shrimati will remain the same if Shrikanth acknowledges her role. His egocentric and domineering demeanour helps her see her errors. She leaves her spouse and goes to another country to get a doctorate in psychology. After a few minutes of thorough consideration of Shrimati's choice in the book, the reader's opinion shifts in favour of it. Only through life's ups and downs can one come to terms with the truth. Shrikant comes to terms with his oversight, but it's too late to correct his course of action.

In sum, Sudha Murty presents the bold, intelligent Shrimati, who faces her life alone. Without any complaints, she accepts her fate, tried to do all her best to the happiness of others, her husband, the greedy in- laws and the guests. She even forgets her own life, her dreams and the right to become a mother. In her every sphere of life, she was perfect, a perfect daughter- in- law, sister- in- law and wife. Shrimati was never excited about her luck and the luxurious life. She was the same Shrimati, the village girl, who always liked the Bakula flowers and her motherland, India. She showed Collins the past glory, the monuments, and the rich heritage of India. While Shrikant was the follower of European culture, the victim of Industrial revolution, and the technocrat could not understand her love for India's rich cultural legacy.

Symbolic meaning in 'Gently Falls the Bakula'

The Bakula Tree is a metaphor for women's lives. Bakula trees may survive for up to one hundred years before dying. Flowers are what draw people to this little, light green tree. It has an intoxicating aroma. A faint scent remains even after the blossoms have dried and become brown. When the tree is in full bloom, the ground underneath it is covered in a carpet of blossoms. Bakula's flowers are a metaphor for women. For the sake of their loved ones, they put their careers on hold. They're like a pillar holding up the house's roof. Work, family, and even the achievement of her spouse might provide them delight. They don't save anything for the future. She is a candle that glows brightly for her family.

Gently falls the Bakula portrays the drudgery life of the female protagonist, Shrimati, who seems to experience the pain from her marriage but her husband Shrikant fails to realize the sacrifice of her life. The Bakula flower is considered a souvenir of their love, even though it would dry up, its fragrance will be same like their love.

As a typical Indian woman she sacrifices her intellectual longings and supports her husband as a submissive wife. Shrimati gives up her passion and ends up as a dutiful wife to her husband, after marriage. By doing this she approves and accepts him with his good and bad. Here the litterateur resembles Shrimati with the character of Bhamati; who sacrificed her whole life to support her sage husband without expecting anything from him. When everyone praises the sage's achievement and failed to notice Bhamati's sacrifice, the sage says as follows: No, Shri, I am perfectly all right, but don't you think we should have children now? We are well settled financially. Both of us are over thirty, and thirty is late for a woman.(GFTB -96)

Shrikant gives all the happiness to his beloved but fails to give real happiness. A woman's life is fulfilled when she bears a child. The society expects a married woman to care for her home and she has to give heir to his family. A childless woman is considered a social stigma. Love and marriage between them sustains when there is mutual trust and respect. Shrikant's dedication towards his work made Shrimati feel lonely and also puts barriers to her desire of becoming a mother. Shrikant does not spend his time with his beloved rather he concentrates on his work even in house. Being lonely, gives her unnecessary thoughts.

Shrimati look at the sea with sorrow and bewilderment. The grief that was in her heart was as deep as the ocean. Despite her arguments and her tears he had not listened to her. (GFTB -150)

Now we turn to another popular work, *House of Cards*.

House of Cards

Burning ambitions, the zeal to succeed and become super rich and powerful in the world is the desire of many, especially the young generation. But will this all spell happiness and peace in the future? Don't really know? It's time you bought for yourself the *House of Cards* by Sudha Murty and gain insights into these important yet crucial matters of life.

Main thread that ran through this novel is that financial riches help to build physical infrastructure but cause the destruction of the close human relations. Mridula chose to marry Dr. Sanjay because she found him honest having a sense of social responsibility. Both of them in the initial phase of their married life had philanthropic intentions and spent some portion of their income in helping the poor and deprived sections of the society. Mridula took up a job to supplement family income so as to enable Sanjay to concentrate on his medical services to the patients in Government hospital. Sanjay started his own hospital which brought him unforeseen success in the field. But influx of easy money spoiled Sanjay and turned him into an unethical medical professional. Money made him insensitive to the significance of humanitarian values in personal life. It hurt Mridula. She gradually drifted away from Sanjay. Mridula left Sanjay in order to save her conscience from corruption. Huge building of hospital and palatial residential quarters collapsed like a baseless house of cards. Sanjay's efforts to bring back Mridula in his life failed miserably because the homeliness of the house had been demolished by lack of mutual faith between the couple.

Sudha Murty as always portrays a serious issue in a simple yet impactful story. *House of Cards* is the journey of Mridula, from being a happy young girl hailing from a small village to a married woman grappling with the ways of life in a metropolitan city. Stories like these are not uncommon in Indian society.

The author has rightly hit the nail on how a woman's sacrifice for her husband and family is considered a moral obligation, as if she lives her life for everyone but herself. *House of Cards* is a story of Mridula, an ambitious young lady hailing from a tiny village in Karnataka who marries Sanjay, a young not so well settled doctor and the couple relocates to Bangalore to realize their dreams. With the passage of time, Mridula realizes the true nature of people, their selfishness, their materialism and narrow idealisms which make people venture on unwanted paths to achieve their goals. As she still feels positive towards her husband and life in general, she does take her challenges quite seriously.

But when Sanjay, her husband starts his private practice which flourishes followed by an increase in money and power, she does become anxious and worrisome. The final straw strikes when Mridula comes to know that Sanjay is no longer the same Sanjay she loved.

The more Mridula sees of the world, the more she realizes how selfish and materialistic people can be. But she does not take the ups and downs of life to heart, and lives each day with positive energy. Trouble brews when Sanjay quits his government job and starts an immensely successful private practice. With affluence comes the never ending ambition for more, and the inevitable slide into corrupt practices.

For a long time, Mridula has no idea that Sanjay has sold his soul; when the truth hits her, she has no recourse but to walk out on him. But can she really find a space of her own?

This intricately woven novel explores human relationships in telling detail, and holds up a mirror to our society with candor and with conviction. It is about how Mridula takes a stand for herself and questions 25 years of her marriage. The strong independent woman arises in such crisis. She doesn't give up on her values.

All of Sudha Murty's books teach you a lesson not like a self help book but by living it through her characters experiences.

THEMES

The novel dealt with two major themes mainly. First one is the destructive effects of money on close domestic relations. The second one is the ascending rate of malpractices in the medical field in India. A protagonist of this novel Sanjay came from a lower middle class Indian family from a semi urban area and became a renowned medical practitioner through incessant hard work. When he worked in a Government medical college in Bangalore as an apprentice, he cared for the patients and their relatives without any expectations. He thought of it as the most noble professions in the world. His idea was that "If he continued in the Government hospital, he could teach the next generation and easily keep himself updated with the latest information about surgery, drugs and other medical breakthroughs. He recollected his father's words; "Sanjay, the foremost duty of a doctor is to take care of his patients. As a doctor, you should understand a patient's sufferings and serve him the same way that you serve God. God doesn't stay in just T. Narasipura's temple. He also comes in the form of a patient." He treated his patients in public hospital with a pious sense of devotion, thinking of them as the incarnations of divine souls. He was available to them for twenty four hours a day, without caring much for his own health. Though he suffered due to the political interferences there, he did not deter from his voluntary selfless services to the poor and needy. He faced many odds there for the sake of his patients. He cared for his beloved wife Mridula and discussed each and every point of his personal and professional career with her. His world comprised of his wife and son in the first phase.

Mridula reciprocated his simplicity, honesty and integrity by continuously showering her love and affection on him. She had opted to marry him in spite of his deformity because he had not hidden it from her. His frankness had impressed her. Even when she knew that life after marriage was going to be a battle, she was ready to fight it out with the help of her Sanjay.

Relationship between Mridula and Sanjay in the initial phase was based on mutual love and trust. They knew each other pretty well. They had woven their destiny in each other's interdependence. This helped them build a palatial house for them and state of the art hospital for the needy patients. But then things began to go wrong. Affluence spoiled their innocence. Sanjay began to play a game of hide and seek with Mridula for no specific reason. Wealth brought arrogance in him which tore him away from Mridula. He imbibed a capitalist's philosophy and said, "Nothing is black or white in this world. The cow gives milk for its calf. But we drink that milk. Isn't that wrong? Trees have life. But we cut them and use their wood. Isn't that wrong too? Mosquitoes and bugs are also creatures. Don't we kill them because they trouble us? Big fish always eats the small fish. Is that wrong?" Mridula was dumbstruck by Sanjay's array of arguments and was forced to revise her thinking about him.

In spite of all professional hurdles in Sanjay's life, their conjugal life was smooth. Lack of money kept them together; needs stuck them to each other. Mridula brought three lakh rupees from her middle-class father to build a hospital. She purposefully avoided a debate with her mother-in-law by giving her undue respect to help Sanjay keep his cool and concentrate on his work. She thought of Sanjay's sister's convenience before her own comforts. Sanjay in return respected Mridula's parents. Everything seemed smooth. Sanjay's ideals however collapsed in the face of incessant flow of unaccountable money in the hospital. He obtained name and fame within such a comparatively short time that he had no need to think about their miserable past. He could not eat on time and rest for a while. The needy patients, international medicine companies and corrupt doctors paid him white and black money. He deliberately kept it a secret from Mridula. He learned to amass money through all the possible sources. Money blinded him. He started blaming Mridula for being sensitive and emotional and philosophized that if she was less emotional she would have better chances of success in life. He made fun of Mridula's monthly salary forgetting its crucial role in shaping his life in the past. He mocked at her wise suggestions to be considerate to his patients. He unscrupulously hid his unethical medical practices in the hospital from his wife. First he ignored her; gradually he began to hide things from her. Later on he began to lie to her about the hospital management. In the end he became arrogant.

All these changes resulted into an unbridgeable gap between the two. Mridula had no place in his busy schedule. "He came home and joined his family for dinner. This was the only time he spent with Shishir. He talked to him about everything and advised him on his future. Mridula did not play an important role anywhere in Sanjay's life. Rosemary assisted Sanjay in the hospital, Shankar managed the accounts, Sakamma did the cooking and Shishir entertained him.

Riches played its diabolic role in breaking them into pieces. Innocent Mridula was profoundly hurt by the changes in Sanjay's attitude to her and to his profession. She tried to reason things out with him but it necessarily ended in unexpectedly humiliating responses from Sanjay. He mocked at her old fashioned thinking. He ridiculed her ignorance about the changes in global scenario. She realized that he was incorrigible and there was only one way out to save herself from the looming disaster and that was to go away from him at her earliest. Money had purchased his soul.

Naturally, he was not expected to track her down after her sudden disappearance. The novel ended with hallucination in which she felt the hand of Sanjay balancing her swing. Wealth had accumulated but men had decayed. The couple was attached to each other as long as their income was proportionate to their daily needs. They fell into pieces immediately after they began to earn in millions. If one compared Sanjay's initial appearance with his appearance after success, one found a striking difference between the two. He was a simpleton to be easily beguiled by the hearsay stories. Mr. Keshav Rao, a co-passenger casually talked about thefts in the train compartments in Hubli. Sanjay took it so seriously that he kept his bag clutched to his chest throughout the remaining journey. The same Sanjay did not care about his wife later. He cooked stories, misguided Mridula on many accounts. He even sent her to a psychiatrist. This shows the undesirable and destructive effect of money on the otherwise plain minds. Success and money had corrupted his entire being.

Traditional marriages that took place not primarily because of love between a boy and girl but because of parents' wish were thought to be a hindrance in the personal development of the both. That is why some scholars and psychologists suggested "love marriages" as a remedy. New arrangement allowed boys and girls to choose their spouse without much interference from the family in particular and society in general. Experience now shows that the so called love marriages have not been successful always. Instead of solving the previous problems, these types of marriages have added new problems to the old ones. Presence of husband's parents in the house was thought to be a stumbling block in the smooth conduct of the lively relations between husband and wife.

They were not free to move around as per their wish. The husband and wife could not go out without parents' permission. Though this was true to some extent, the bond between husband and wife remained intact under the presence of the elders in the family. New type of marriages through personal acquaintance has given much needed space to the couple. They are allowed to discuss and plan their future within themselves. They can have a new group of friends and friendship with the people of their choice. Each one of them can take up a job as per his/her convenience and aptitude. In spite of all such freedom, so called love marriages in India do not seem to be successful. Boy and girl seem to misread the difference between liberty and liberation. Bell Daniel writes, "While the 19th century emphasized 'liberty' the idea of being free of inscriptive ties, the 20th century emphasizes 'liberation' ad being free from all institutional restrains."

Mridula's son Shishir did not care much for his mother because he had always seen her as a middle-class wage earner. He had seen his father earning lakhs of rupees every month and also knew the purchasing power of money in human market. He purchased clothes, electronic gadgets, furniture and food items at exorbitant rates without thinking much about their need in life. When Mridula tried to explain to him the importance of good habits, he made a mockery of her profession. He knew that once one had tremendous wealth, human relations were meaningless. Young generation's thoughts about the place of money in life are vividly expressed in Shishir's ideas about his mother. "Amma was so beautiful when she was young. Had she been taller, she could have entered the Miss India pageant. She has wasted her beauty by becoming a teacher and housewife. Had I been in her place, I'd have pursued modeling and probably made more money than dad and taken less time than him. She could have become a lady doctor and joined dad and they could have built many more nursing homes together. Amma would have been also famous. She's spent so much of energy on teaching children in Government schools."

This remark showed that Shishir looked at Mridula not as mother but as a contestant in beauty competition. The title *House of Cards* signified the rickety nature of human relations in the modern world. It is always said in India that houses are not built merely by lifeless bricks, cement and steel. They are built by trust among the members of the house. If members did not possess mutual love, it became a rickety house of cards, likely to collapse at the slightest thump.

Members of Indian families are intricately connected to each other. Husband, wife, son, daughter, grandparents, grandsons, uncle, aunts are closely weaved in personal relations. Any threat to such relations always causes sleepless nights to the sensitive minds. Mridula and Anita were flabbergasted by the money madness of their husbands. They were shocked by the careless attitude of their sons to their mothers. Marriage between Sanjay and Mridula lacked the seriousness of legal contract and piousness of sacred *sanskara*. So it fell apart like a house of cards. They did love each other deeply initially. Once they came to know each other fully well, too much of acquaintance tore them from each other. It was a psychological truth that a person can not consistently like or dislike one thing or a person with the same degree of passion for a long time. Principle of diminishing utility in Economics which is generally applied to personal taste was applicable in close relations as well.

In this narrative, Mridula, a young woman from a hamlet in Karnataka, tells of her aspirations to become a doctor. Sanjay, a young doctor, introduces her to a new world. They get married and make Bangalore their home. A deeper understanding of human selfishness and materialism emerges as she spends more time in the business sector. She has a positive outlook on life despite the ups and downs that come her way. As soon as she arrived in Karnataka, she began her new job and life as a teacher. Sanjay made less than her. Sanjay handed Mridula his income as soon as they were married and instructed her to handle it. She meticulously tracked every rupee that passed through her hands. They were content with the earnings they'd racked up. On the other hand, Lakshmi, Sanjay's sister, is a squanderer. While she's married to a typical clerk, he makes his living by accepting bribes. They like flaunting their money. In their large mansion, they had everything, even extravagantly expensive furnishings. Their nature and location will be altered later on.

When Sanjay resigned from the government and started a private practise, her woes increased significantly. She serves as a pillar of support for him. She's right there with her, holding his hand as he makes his way up the mountain. For the purpose of opening a care home, they've both taken out loans. For the sake of her husband's financial well-being, she pawned her jewellery. She doesn't like squandering money. No auto rickshaw for her, and she has no interest in buying more saris. Starting a new care facility went very well, and money started pouring in. Sanjay's desire to gain more and more leads him to engage in unscrupulous actions as a result of his increased wealth. Because of his desire for power and money, their relationship suffers.

The husband and wife are on opposite sides of the tracks. Her beloved Sanjay is no longer Sanjay to Mridula. She has come to the conclusion that she can no longer be in a relationship with him. She flees from Karnataka and returns to her home in the countryside.

Mythology: The major Indian epics are the *Ramayana* and the *Mahabharata.* You'll be able to connect the dots back to Sita, the great *Ramayana* heroine. Sita is said to be the adopted daughter of the monarch Janaka and the daughter of the soil goddess Bhumi. She weds Rama, the prince of Ayodhya, in a *syamvara*, a Hindu ritual of marriage. After her marriage, she and her husband and brother-in-law are exiled to the jungle. Rakshasa Ravana, the ruler of Lanka, kidnaps her. Until Rama frees her, she is held captive in Ashoka vana. After the conflict, Rama refuses to marry her. Sita enters the flames as a test of her holiness.

God Agni is afraid to even look at her. It demonstrates her innocence and total devotion to Rama. They return to Ayodhya and are crowned king and queen. Rama, on the other hand, is willing to take a risk with her own life. Rama abandons a pregnant Sita since it is his responsibility to do so. Sita gives birth to twins Lava and Kusha in the hermitage of Sage Valmiki. With the help of the sage, she nourishes and binds them together. Sita no longer desires to control the country, despite Rama and his people realising their error. To her dismay, she returns to the earth's womb. Comparison of the two novels: Between the two books, there is less of a divide. Shrimati and Mridula were raised in small villages. In contrast, one is a teacher while the other is pursuing an academic career. They prioritise spending time with their loved ones. Both women have been abused and abandoned by their spouses. There is, however, a little difference in their duties.

Mridula is stuck in a rut and can't get out of it. She takes him back, but Shrimati makes him understand that what's gone is lost. Males are expected to demonstrate equal devotion and care for their wives and families in patriarchal societies, but they should also be aware that they have an obligation to do so. The patriarchal system has ruled for millennia. Similarities may be found in the characters of Sita in the *Ramayana*, Shrimati in *Gentle Falling the Bakula*, Mridula in *House of Cards*, and many other women's characters. Women are just like this. They are recognised for their patience, intelligence, and submission. It's quite impossible to get close to them after they have lost their cool and reacted.

In sum, post- modern women have broken the walls of restrictions and traditional prejudices. They unravel the fact that very few are ready to wipe the tears of suffering women in the name of socio-cultural tradition, which by the way is made by the interest and profit of men. Mridula and Shrimati typified the life of post-modern world, even though they face the tribulations and humilitations. Like the females in a feminist world they do not keep silent. As post-modern females they come out of their worries and build a new life which gives them real happiness as well as an individual identification. Post-modern feminism acknowledges them as an asset, and proves women are not helpless and dependent.

To represent post-modernism the protagonist's life does not end, rather it starts from the decision she has taken. Education helps them to take a decision. Woman is more capable than man; it clearly shows that in the present age women have to realize their capacity. The suppressed protagonists get frustrated and try to prove themselves; in this process a woman has to undergo a series of humiliation, betrayals to make her life cheerful. Post-modern women perceived education as an asset which makes their world positive.

Sudha Murty, being a woman knew the emotional makeup of females well. As she has mentioned in her telephonic talk with the researcher, she had taken tremendous efforts to portray these emotions in her works well. She knew that teenager girls in India can be easily beguiled into friendship and then can be emotionally blackmailed and exploited to selfish purposes by men. Kate Millet observes, "The concept of Romantic Love affords a means of emotional manipulation which the male is free to exploit, since love is the only circumstance in which the female is ideologically pardoned for sexual activity. And convictions of romantic love are convenient to both parties since it is often the only condition in which the female can overcome the far more powerful conditioning she has received towards sexual inhibitions. Romantic love also observes the realities of female status and burden of economic dependency."

Second theme of the novel is the alarmingly growing rate of corruption in globalizing India. Money in modern India has acquired the position of omnipresent, omniscient and omnipotent God. It has replaced all traditional values like faith, pity, love, peace, affection, sympathy, compassion, sacrifice etc. by capitalistic values like competition, profit, gains, lies etc. People have begun to believe that for being successful in life, there is no substitute to money. As a result, we come across rampant corruption in social, political, commercial, medical and professional fields. Sanjay who once visualized Gods and Goddesses in his patients in Government hospital suddenly began to treat them as a machine to mint money. "When Sanjay saw a list of patients and their scheduled operations for the day, he remembered his father's words; "See Gods in your patients" Yes, he did see God— Goddess Lakshmi in fact. Every patient was a source of income to him." This novel threw light on the hideous practices in Government, semi-Government and private establishments in India in order to earn more money.

Sanjay worked in Government hospital in Bangalore with utmost dedication and zeal. He treated patients with maximum care and minimum inconvenience to them. He spent almost twenty four hours of a day in the services of needy patients in the hospital. The same Sanjay was victimized by the political pressures of the health department of the Government. Minister Napalingegowda's daughter-in-law did not conceive for many years after marriage. When she ultimately did, doctors tried to pass the buck of her complicated delivery to other doctor in order to escape probable risk in the case. Sanjay was strategically assigned the duty to look after her safe delivery. Innocent Sanjay had no other thought except the one of patient's safety. He succeeded in his job. But the entire credit for the child and mother's good health was passed on to Dr. Lata to please her IAS father. When Sanjay expressed his displeasure over the discriminatory treatment in Government services, Alex told him, "Sanjay, my logic is different. Let's assume that you get a salary of ten thousand rupees. Half of that is to accept the injustice around you and the other half is for your actual work. If you don't still understand that, then you're foolish".

World Health Organization (WHO) had arranged a three week seminar on AIDS in the USA for Government doctors in India. Sanjay wanted to attend it in order to acquire fresh knowledge and new skills in the treatment of AIDS. He was the only person qualified for representing Karnataka state in the seminar. He was made to run from pillar to post in search of a sponsor. When the final list reached him, he was shocked to see strange names there. The minister had recommended another doctor of his favour. Kempunanjamma had been a VIP patient. She delivered a baby girl. Nanjamma, an ordinary woman on the adjacent cot had delivered a baby boy. Dr. Saroja switched the babies to win the favour of the minister. Kempunanjamma got a baby boy and Nanjamma got a baby girl. When Sanjay exposed her treacherous game, he was transferred from Bangalore to Bellur. Pharmaceutical companies played a foul role in deciding the medical policies of the Government. They bribed the ministers, administrative bureaucrats and executive officers to prescribe their medicine brands in the Government hospitals. Nobody in the system thought about the probable risk involved in substandard medical and surgical treatment to helpless patients. In case of mass casualty innocent doctors were punished.

Appointments of doctors, their promotions and sponsorships were always manipulated by ministers in consultation with national and multinational medicine companies. They had their commission agents in regular hospital staff that kept informing them about the daily happenings in the hospital.

Sanjay suffered heavily during his job in Government hospital at Bangalore. Unfortunately, the same Sanjay was trapped into the net of malpractices in his own private practice later on. Sanjay started Sushrut Nursing Home with the monetary help of Mridula's father. He followed the ethical practices prescribed by medical council in the beginning. But he soon succumbed to the pressures of market economy. He hiked consultation fees from fifty rupees to hundred rupees simply because somebody casually told him that enhanced fees implied additional value for the doctor. He did C-section even when normal delivery was possible. He forced medicine companies to pay him heavy commission. He thought, "By recommending Prakash's products, I must also gain something. If two similar products from two different companies are equally good, then I should think of what is advantageous for me. In any business, a win-lose situation equals exploitation. And if it is win-lose, it's plain foolishness." He advised his son Shishir to start infertility centre exclusively for rich patients because they could afford to pay handsomely. "Sanjay had snubbed Mridula and said, "This is not a temple. We have to give our patients whatever they need. After all they are paying us. Please don't try to teach me moral science." Instead of freeing himself from the dreadful clutches of the past, he became a prey to it. It was difficult for him to free himself from the giant wheels of free economy in India. He did not mind bluffing to Mridula.

CHARACTERIZATION

Significantly Mridula and Sanjay are the two major characters of this novel. Ratnamma, Lakshami, Alex and Anita played auxiliary roles in the action of the novel.

Mridula

In fact, Mridula is a protagonist of *House of Cards*. The entire novel revolved around her actions, reactions, feelings and emotions. When we came across her for the first time, we were impressed by her wisdom and maturity in her early twenties. Writer described her as "Mridula was not like everybody, she was different. She had enormous enthusiasm for life and unlimited energy for reading, cooking and sketching. She wanted to spend every minute of the day fruitfully. It seemed that the sun rose for her and the rainbow colours were meant only for her. Every day was to be lived its fullest and every beautiful minute to be enjoyed." Mridula had been a studious girl in her school days. Her teachers wanted her to join courses either in medicine or in engineering in order to do justice to her talent and industriousness. They wished her to go abroad to earn dollars there. She, however, was bent on becoming a teacher because teaching was her hobby. It was her vocation.

This proved that she had a mature head on her young shoulders. Teacher in her could face difficulties in her married life with Sanjay later. Teaching had groomed her into a wise, considerate and selfless woman who thought about other's comforts and convenience first. In her adolescence, Mridula was impressed not so much by Sanjay's academic degrees as by his utter simplicity and child like honesty. She worshiped his virtues and was not drawn towards his masculinity. She accepted Sanjay as her husband along with his deformity. When her father informed her about his short hand, she replied "If Sanjay met with an accident that left him handicapped after we got married, then you would not hold that against him. So I don't have any objection to the alliance if both of you are ok with it." This affirmed her conviction that she was not after looks and riches of the boy she wanted to get married with. She wanted a boy with plain heart and clear head as her husband.

A characteristic feature, Mridula carried a social sense right from her adolescence to her womanhood. Her village did not have medical facilities. She completed a special training in first aid treatment and gave injections to the injured people and pregnant ladies there. She worked as a volunteer in maternity home for the safe delivery of village women. When Sanjay started his own hospital, she advised Sanjay to render free services to slum-dwellers and treatment at concessional rates to needy poor patients. Her roots in the soil were so deeply ingrained that financial success in the later part of their life did not blind her. She had a conscience which guided Sanjay to keep his cool in his difficult times. She helped him proactively to overcome the feeling of utter frustration when the Government hospital politics victimized him. She used the entire amount of her salary to repay the house loan. "I don't mind. As long as you earn money legally and ethically, I'm with you. I'll help you in your struggle. You can earn money illegally too, but I'll never approve of that." She never bothered Sanjay for daily house hold expenses. She wanted her Sanjay to be successful both as a human being and also as a medical practitioner. Mridula had a mature head on her young shoulders. Whenever Sanjay was disturbed by the hospital politics, she helped him overcome the feeling of uneasiness in him. Mridula worked as an antidote to Sanjay's ailments.

She knew that Sanjay would be lost without her moral support. She was therefore proactive in domestic affairs. When Sanjay was unjustly transferred from Bangalore to Belur, she courageously looked after her son, herself and also her husband. Mridula maintained considerable respect for herself and her Sanjay in the first phase of their married life. She did not want to endanger Sanjay's reputation by borrowing money from friends and relatives. She told Sanjay, "Sanjay, I have gold jewellery that my parents gave me during our wedding. I don't wear much gold anyway. I can sell it. I'll ask Appa for some money too. We can borrow the remaining amount from bank. But we will not take any money from Alex." This gesture showed her spirit of sacrifice for Sanjay. Generally Indian women hesitate to do away with gold jewellery given to them by their parents. But Mridula did the supreme sacrifice.

Her parents were not very rich, yet she managed to borrow three lakh rupees from her father for the construction of a hospital. The same Mridula was completely broken when her trust in Sanjay was thwarted by her own Sanjay, who followed unethical practices in his personal and professional life. He hiked consultation fee from fifty to hundred rupees just to gain pseudo satisfaction of being regarded an expert. He performed C-section operations even when they were not required. His shady deals with medicine companies and medical representatives disturbed her to the core.

Sanjay

Another significant character in the novel is Sanjay. His first appearance was unimpressive. He was constantly aware of his short arm. He carefully kept himself away from public eye due to a nagging sense of inferiority complex in him due to his deformity. He was so unfamiliar with the ways of the world then that he believed copassenger's story of rail robbers as true, which kept him awake throughout the journey. The writer described his conduct in the following words, "Sanjay was not a seasoned traveller. So he was shocked listening to Keshav Rao. He was scared that if he lost the small bag with his clothes, he would have to attend the wedding in his *baniyan* and *loongi* too. He picked his small bag from the floor and kept it under his head so that it would be safe and he could use it as a pillow for the rest of the trip too." The above paragraph showed that he feared everything around him and doubted everybody in the crowd.

His timid attitude to life was an outcome of two important factors in his life. First, one of his arms was shorter than the other arm. Sanjay had fallen from the tree when he was just five. Lack of proper treatment left him handicapped forever. Sanjay himself narrated the story of his deformity to Mridula not for invoking sympathy, but to be honest with a friend like her. He wrote a letter to Mridula "I don't want to lie to you. I come from a poor family. We have some land but I don't have any other asset. I do not have a father. My sister is already married. I am not equal to you in looks or money. You already know about my hand. But I am hard working and honest. I want to spend the rest of my life with you. If you feel the same way about me, then write back. Otherwise destroy this letter and forget about it."

He gave information about himself and his family to Mridula through letter before he proposed to her. The letter presented the child like innocence of Sanjay to Mridula. It clearly showed the factual self-assessment by Sanjay with honest intentions and to present his case to a girl he wished to marry. The same plain, sincere and honest Sanjay remained before us till the time he started his own maternity home in

Bangalore. He treated patients in the Government hospital in Bangalore with a single minded devotion to serve the poor and underprivileged patients. Neither the social status nor the political position of the patients came in his way to serve the patients. He willingly worked for three nights a week when other doctors on the staff excused themselves from their night duties.

Though he was aware of the dangers involved in such initiatives, his only aim then was to serve and earn patients blessings. He handled the complicated delivery cases with skill and feel. He advised the patients in the Government hospital to wait for natural delivery rather than straightway going in for C-section. He was too innocent to get into hospital politics then. Sanjay had always been victimized by his seniors and hospital administration in Bangalore. Yet he did not retaliate because he believed in the humane aspects of medical profession. He carried no grudge against the patients in the Government hospital. As far as the treatment was concerned, he never discriminated between VIP and ordinary patients. It was Mridula who persuaded him to commence private practice in Bangalore in order to enable Sanjay to carry on with his philanthropic ideas without the interference of others.

He had faced Government hospital politics without surrendering to it. There are some people who believed that their decision to start private practice was directed by their desire to earn money. But it was not true. Their first and foremost aim then was to go away from the filthy atmosphere in the Government job. There was an unbelievable change in him after the unforeseen success in his hospital. The circumstances taught him to lie, to take up unethical practice and to hide facts from his own wife. He learned the ways of the world in a new setup. He sold his soul to outside forces in order to amass wealth.

He hid many things from Mridula in the later part of his married life. He opened bank accounts secretly without the knowledge of Mridula, transferred money to the accounts of his sister and mother without informing his wife. He increased consultation fees from nominal fifty to hefty hundred and fifty rupees in order to bloat his ego. He entered shady deals with pharmaceutical companies in order to make black money. He performed caesarian operations even when they were not required. C. Kilmer Myers wrote, "A real parish is a wondrously beautiful web of human relationship which is given meaning by the man who is Himself the meaning of life." Thus, Dr. Sanjay became a commercial tycoon and in the process went away from the innate nobility of his heart. His tirade, "Yes, whatever I think is right. That's the reason for my success. What do you know about real life? Your world is limited to your school. Look at my colleagues. They're still rotting in Government service. But look at me. I made the right decision at the right time. I've been successful without anybody's help," threw light on his egoist self.

He repented his behavior with Mridula and surrendered to her once again. He held a string of Mridula's swing with one hand trying to support her. Sanjay realized his mistakes and tried to mend them. Though the novel ended in suspense, it seemed that Mridula would accept his apology. The house will be rebuilt. Sanjay is Indian in person and spirit. He had been severely affected by bizarre thinking in the past. He would surely go back to his roots. Question may be raised to ask whether Sanjay changed due to his sorrowful and harrowing experiences at Government hospital or because of the influx of bad money and unaccountable wealth in his life. Sudha Murty has shown through out her writing that money spoiled the person. Illegitimate income caused a downward slide in the moralilty of people. When one was earning barely enough to suffice daily needs, one didn't give too much importance to it. However, too much of money consumed the person. This is exactly what happened to Sanjay in the second phase of his career.

NARRATIVE TECHNIQUE

We have come across the salient features of narrative technique of Sudha Murty in the introductory chapter of this book. Sudha Murty's narrative style in this novel resembled the simple and straightforward narrative style of "There was a king. . ." kind of the narrative technique of the past. She described physical features of characters, various events and incidents in their life, their locations in such a simple language that readers are reminded of grandma's tales to grandchildren at the bedtime. She has used following narrative techniques to weave the story and plot of this novel.

Use of Coincidence

As in her other novels, Sudha Murty made use of chance elements in the meeting and marriage of Mridula and Dr. Sanjay in this novel. Sanjay had gone to his friend's wedding at Hubli. Mridula was there at the same place to attend her friend Surekha's wedding. As it happens in small places like Hubli in India, electricity supply stopped all of a sudden leaving the entire wedding centre in panicky gloom. Considerate Mridula ran from pillar to post with a match box to light candles in the dark rooms. Sanjay who had heard of the small thefts in the area during his travel in train was taken aback by the entry of an unknown figure in the room. He grabbed the unfamiliar hand of Mridula with the eureka sense that he had been able to catch the thief. Writer has described this incident in the following words. "It was dark and for a minute, Mridula was scared. The person did not budge or let go off her hand. Then came a harsh male voice; "I caught you".

Village vs. City

Another significant feature of her narrative technique is the use of contrast between village and city culture. Mridula and Sanjay both came from villages and shifted to cosmopolitan city like Bangalore. In spite of her continuous contacts with national and international cities, Sudha Murty seemed to believe that villagers are more reliable than city dwellers; that villagers are innocent, simple, straightforward and honest; rural Indian life is still pure and pious. Mridula came from Aladhalli and Sanjay came from Narsipura. Murty described the natural beauty of both the places but did not do so for big cities. This helped her carry forward her ideas that villages only would maintain the divine beauty of human life.

Use of Flashback

Sudha Murty used a famous flash back technique in this novel repeatedly. Mridula led her childhood life in the calm surroundings in village happily. Though careful, she had no prolonged worries. She never confronted a situation whereby she had to question her future. The same Mridula was nostalgic of the carefree life in her village of the past. She remembered the golden days she had spent with her parents and friends in Aladhalli. Sanjay lived a simple life in his childhood in the lanes and alleys of Narasipura. The same Sanjay remembered his past with her mother. He earned truckloads of wealth but the same wealth had deprived him of simple pleasures of everyday life. He could not eat on time, could not sleep with ease. Such pressure situations forced them to find relief in their past.

Epistolary Method

Writing a letter, sending a message with cloud or a duck is an old technique of intercommunication in the old Indian literature. The language and content of Sanjay's letter demonstrated Sanjay's cautious attitude and careful approach to the whole affair. It contained the modest declaration of his property and honest appeal to accept him in spite of his deformity. He also appealed to Mridula to keep the letter secret if she wished to decline his proposal. Thus the carefully calculated words and syntax of the old times are seen in her narrative technique here.

Binary Division of Characters

Significantly here Sudha Murty has created a binary division in main characters. Sanjay and Mridula became two opposite ends of the same stick in the later part of their life. Sanjay was spoiled by the tremendous income in his hospital. Mridula on the hand did not go astray from good qualities. Once corruption entered Sanjay's mind, it killed the very springs of humanitarian beliefs in him. Mridula remained the same throughout, before and after economic riches. Sudha Murty juxtaposed these characters in order to create and increase the dramatic conflict between humanity and inhumanity, between good and bad. Indian philosophy believed in the Karma theory which said that the sins accumulated through unethical means have DNA effect on the children also. Shishir's condition in England certainly had something to do with his father"s unlawful practices. Sudha Murty has presented another binary distinction through the characters of Alex and Anita. Anita had got married with Alex simply for her love for him.

Suggestive End

Characteristically the author ended this novel on a suspense note. Mridula was completed disillusioned in her life with Sanjay who had changed to the diametrically opposite direction during the twenty five years of their togetherness. Mridula had preserved her innate qualities like simplicity, innocence and honesty for a considerable time. She expected the same from her Sanjay. But he had belied her hopes and she was devastated. He earned money at the cost of hard earned social prestige which forced Mridula to leave him.

The same Mridula, however, was shown in mood to reconcile with Sanjay. She fantasized that Sanjay had held her swing on which she was sitting with one 'good' hand. The end showed the divided mind of Mridula. She thought of help from Sanjay on the one hand and on the other hand she had left that hand behind. Whether she repented her previous decision and hoped to rectify it is not clear from the end. As such, the novel remained open ended.

Weaknesses in Narration

As is obvious, Sudha Murty lacked the natural style of extended narration, resultantly her writing became a hotch-potch assemblage of separate incidents and comments. The best narrative technique comprised of gradual ascendance to the peak, followed by climax and then gradual downward slide and the final end. George Orwell's *Animal Farm*, Raja Rao's *Serpent and the Rope*, Khushawant Singh's *Train to Pakistan* are some of the perfect novels which build the tension and gradually release it. There are some minor flaws in her narrative technique. Sudha Murty sometimes takes a sudden leap in her narration without convincing reasons.

Sudha Murty took a sudden leap in chapter number eighteen "Money Brings Changes" by forcing the time to race forward by fourteen years. In fact the first fourteen years had been the most noticeable years in the life of Mridula's family. Both of them together had built the empire. Sanjay was recognized as the most successful gynecologist in Bangalore. Mridual's dream of life had come true with a son and a luxurious four bed room flat. Writer could have described the story of their incessant struggle and success in a chapter or two. Sudha Murty did not do it. She described it all within a paragraph of about six lines in the following way. "Fourteen years had passed since the nursing home had been started and Sushruta Nursing Home had now become one of the leading maternity homes in Bangalore. Many people had written Sanjay off before but now, he had become a role model. He had progressed in leaps and bounds, amassed a fortune and made a name for himself."

It can be concluded that *House of Cards* is a traditional novel based on the traditional theme that money corrupted the holy homely relations between husband and wife. Liberalization of Indian economy opened the floodgates of opportunities for Indians. Indians who believed in the irreversible role of fate and providence in shaping the common human life gradually began to believe in the continuous hard work and careful planning of personal and family affairs. Indian youth picked the gauntlet of challenges involved in competition and progress. But unfortunately, the same youth lost the very foundations of human relations. The old Indian culture adhered to old cultural values like respect, mutual trust, sacrifice etc. New commercial world eclipsed the old values. As a result money acquired the all important place of God. It replaced most of the things that represented good and virtuous in the close relations.

Migration of bodies invariably meant the creation and extension of distance between two minds. Mridula accepted to get married with Sanjay for his sincerity and simplicity. Sanjay proposed Mridula to accept him as her husband because he had found her reasonable and compassionate. The same couple fell apart as the walls of house of cards with the flow of money. Anita was right when she told Mridula, "Mridula, do you know that when men get more money than they need, their wife begins to look ugly to them? They think that they could have done better. They forget that they were nothing when their wife married them and that she has stayed loyal to them through their ups and downs."

Summing Up

To conclude, the novel showed the harmful effects of insatiable hunger for money in modern times. Mridula and Dr. Anand began their life well through mutual sacrifice. They faced poverty, humiliation and challenges together to prove themselves right to the world around them. As soon as they settled into comfortable coexistence, incoming money began to play its foul role in their life. Mridula was disturbed and hurt by the irrational accumulation of wealth by Sanjay. She sanctioned some time to him to rectify his mistakes. But her condition in life worsened day by day when her son also joined the race. She had no other way but to leave the sinful house decorated by Sanjay through exploitation of the needy patients. Their house collapsed like a house of cards. The novel also showed Indian peoples' inability to cope with riches.

Sudha Murty has shown that the use of simple words may also be used to convey thoughts and perspectives. The relevance or talent of a piece of literature doesn't necessarily need the use of esoteric terminology or terms. In terms of comprehension, Sudha Murty's writings are so accessible that they become a topic of interest for any reader. The audience and the tale form a strong connection very quickly.

Writing or narration may benefit from this. This shows Sudha Murthy's passion and effectiveness in presenting stories and conveying concepts. In all of her works, Sudha Murty expresses her thoughts clearly. She communicates her ideas in plain language. 'Unlike the older and classical authors, whose use of language befuddles contemporary readers, Sudha Murty is a breeze to get through. Her words are devoid of cliches and clichéd terms.' Traditional Indian ladies have not changed even after their country gained freedom. She is a social outcast because of her vulnerability and emotional numbness. She is bound by the shackles of tradition, both within and publicly. She has a hard time adjusting to the realities of daily life. Women in the present period are also violent and sad as a result of the continual torture in the household and outside, therefore they are unable to deal with other people.

References

Bell, Daniel (1980), The Winding Passage. Cambridge, ABT Books, 1980. P. 161.

Chakravarty, Joya (2003), *Indian Writing in English, Perspectives*, New Delhi: Atlantic Publishers and Distributors.

Eagleton, Mary, ed. (1986), Feminist Literary Theory: A Reader, BlackWell.

Iyengar, Shrinivasa (1983), Indian writing in English. New Delhi: Sterling.

Mehrotra, Arvind Krishna (ed) (2003), *A History of Indian Literature in English*, New York: Columbia University Press.

Millet, Kate (2000), *Sexual Politics*, Urbana, University of Illinois Press, p. 37.

Mukhopadhyay, Arpita (2018), *Feminism*. Hyderabad: Orient Blackswan Private Limited.

Murty, Sudha (2007), Mahashweta. New Delhi. Penguin Books.

Murty, Sudha (2008), Gently Falls the Bakula, New Delhi. Penguin Books.

Murty, Sudha (2013), House of Cards. New Delhi, Penguin Books India. p. 101

8

Grandma's Bag of Stories and Grandparents Bag of Stories

"Who is the best friend to a man and a woman?" The answer is: "A wife to her husband and a husband to his wife."- Sudha Murty

For most of us, grandparents telling us stories during the holidays have a special place in our memories. The warmth of grandparents' spinning tales that held us rapt is unforgettable. Sudha Murty's *Grandma's Bag of Stories* is just as charming.

Grandma's Bag of Stories

This collection of stories published in 2012 by Penguin Books India is a wonderful collection of tales told by her grandmother and recollected by Sudha Murty when she herself became a grandmother. The book demonstrates a traditional way of grandmother narrating stories to children after dinner, under the milky night sky, with a cold breeze blowing, children feeling drowsy while listening to the stories with innocence reigning all over.

Anand, Krishna, Meena and Raghu arrive at their grandparents' place in Shiggaon. Ajji's and Ajja's house was all readied up for their arrival, with Ajji preparing their favourite snacks. The perfect holiday with wonderful food, fun times with the animals in Ajji-Ajja's house and best of all, the wonderful stories that Ajji told them. After all, when Grandma opens her bag, everyone gathers around.

From her bag, emerges tales of kings and cheats, monkeys and mice, scorpions and treasure, and princesses and onions. Unlikely combinations, one might think, but when Grandma is the one telling them, they are just perfect! The book is great for young children to be read to, and for older children (5+, perhaps) to read for themselves. The whole setting takes us back to our childhood. The school holidays when we would all travel to our grandparents and had this wonderful time with our cousins.

Grandma's Bag of Stories is a beautiful collection of interesting stories to share with kids from the pen of very popular author Sudha Murty. The book will take you through the memory lane of your childhood days spent at your grandparent's home. Sudha Murty's *Grandma's Bag of*

Stories is simply wonderful and full of engaging stories of monkeys and mice, kings and cheats, scorpions and hidden treasures and princesses and onions.

The book starts with the grandmother Ajji waiting for her grandkids Raghu and Meenu to arrive for summer vacations. The other pair of sibling Anand and Krishna had already arrived. The craziness and fondness of the kids for their Ajji is what is narrated in the first chapter of the book. How the kids love to listen to Ajji's funny and wonderful stories.

The conversation between Ajji and her grandchildren is interesting and engaging. It lets us dig into the kind of bondings and inspiration grandparents can have on today's younger generation.

The book takes you on a journey from a real world to the world of fantasies and fiction. The children in the story learn about the village life, farmers, birds, and animals while walking in the paddy fields with their grandfather. On the other hand, they learn about the moral values, culture and different virtues of life from the stories narrated to them by their loving and affectionate grandmother.

Murty's book takes us back to the good old days in which children were molded into decent ways of conduct in the family itself. Elderly people played the role of trainers in such institutions. Her lap worked as the educational psychology lab and her eyes performed the role of a projector of her love, affection and concern for her children. Murty, through her stories, has been successful in recreating that atmosphere in the twenty-first century. There are grandparents, parents, grandchildren, relatives, neighbours and family friends in these narratives. Women busy themselves in making *papadams* and *masalas* during the daytime. Male members of the family are out in the field the whole day. The enchanting nights set against the drowsy hot afternoons therefore provided the perfect background setting to grandma's stories. There are animals, birds, fairies, supernatural beings in her stories.

Here it is worth-mentioning that one of the most important features of these stories is the creation of the child's world. Their preference to the world of fantasy rather than to the world of reality is reasonably taken care of by the writer. It is not that children do not like their parents, it is not that they want to go away from them, its not that children are unaware of their own world, but they like to be transported away from their surrounding atmosphere to an imaginary dream land. When they listen to these stories, they are cut off from actual world to inhabit world of make- believe.

Let's peep through these stories one by one.

Doctor Doctor shows the healthy rewards of charitable social work and undesirable outcome of greedy intents. There is a story of magic pitcher which shows the diabolic effects of greed. Ravi served water to an old man to quench his thirst in the hot summer afternoon. As a result, the water from pitcher got a magic gift to cure diseases. Ravi served the humanitarian purpose by serving water to people free of charge. This went on for some time. After some days Ravi began to charge money for water. Immediately, the pitcher dried. Its magic touch vanished. Sudha Murty has shown the importance of charitable intentions in donations through this story.

Kavery and the Thief shows the significance of presence of mind in senior citizens. There is another story which shows the importance of courageous presence of mind in the face of impending danger. A man came to an old lady with an intention to cheat her. The lady coaxed him to dig her field saying that there were gold coins underneath. When he failed to trace any coin in the field she requested him to pull down the house walls to procure wealth. Unable to get the coins there, she persuaded him to go to the forest. Had she been frightened, the thief would have robbed her of her valuables.

Who is the Happiest of Them All tells us the importance of contentment in life. When the King asked some of his courtiers whether they were happy, all of them answered in positive. The King then permitted them all to collect whatever they liked from his garden. Surprisingly, everybody assiduously grabbed everything that they could lay hands on. "Chandan turned to him and said, "Your majesty, I hope you now realize that people's contentment does not end with having food or money. They also need to be truly happy inside. Only then will they not be swayed when they gain or lose wealth. That is a lesson that everyone, whether King or commoner needs to remember."

Similarly *The Enchanted Scorpions* reveals the practical knowledge of the people from old generation. A man before his death put all his jewels in the lower compartment of box and scorpions in the upper compartment. When a stranger opened the box, scorpions attacked him. He ran away from the box. A member of the family knew that his wise father must have kept something valuable in it. He opened the lower box instead of upper box and received a bag of gold coins.

Horse Trap is about the shortsightedness of immature people. A man saw horse dung and came to the conclusion that within a period of hundred years or so, the world will be filled only with horse dung. He did not see the possibility of the invention of the vehicles like a motor car, train, ship and aero plane which would replace the horses. People should know that every problem has solution. There is absolutely no need to get panicky. Story ended with a lesson that, "If man did not innovate and experiment, our species would have died out, just like George had predicted."

Ill begotten money invariably in the end leads to ill effects is brought forward in *A Treasure for Ramu.* Ramu and Rani got a treasure of gold in the farm land. The couple went mad over the money and went on spending freely without restraint. They squandered all their money like water. Consequently, a time came when they had no money to spend even for their daily needs. They reverted to the poverty of the old times.

The Donkey and the Stick shows the difference between image and reality. People worship stone images without going deep into their significance. There were images of a donkey and a stick. People venerated them like Gods. Once a wise man took a stick and removed the stone to find out the secret of the place. To his surprise, he found a pot of gold under it. Story shows the importance of inquisitiveness in human life.

What's in it for Me puts light on the sorrowful end of crooked mind. A mouse gave a dry twig to a potter in return for a pumpkin. He gave the pumpkin to milkman and took a cow from him. Later on he handed over the cow to the father of a bride for making *kheer* in the wedding party and took the bride. The bride was smarter than the mouse. She cajoled him to enter the hole first. As soon as he got into it she put a big stone on the mouth of a hole. Lesson that Murty wants to teach is that "Always remember that there are wiser people than you. They are likely to outshine you".

The Princess' New Clothes is an allegorical story in which Murty delineates the uselessness of pompous show in life. The Goddess had gifted a child to a King with a warning that the Princess should wear a new piece of cloth everyday. If she failed to change her dress everyday she would die. Beena the princess followed the instructions for many years. One day she saw a girl who looked exceptionally charming because of her simple clothes. Beena was tempted to exchange her new dress for her old sari. No sooner did she change her clothes than she was on her way to death. Story shows the futility of capitalistic madness for beauty.

The Story of Pann shows the emergence of immortal memory through love and sacrifice. Bhanu and Veer were two brothers. They loved each other so much that one could not think of living without the other. When they grew up, Veer joined the army with a noble intention to serve the nation. Unfortunately, he could not be contacted for a long time. So Bhanu and his wife Bharati went on a mission to search for him. They got the information that Veer was killed in the war. Unable to bear the loss, both husband and wife killed themselves. Bhanu became a tree and Bharati a creeper hugging the tree. After some days, Veer came searching for his brother. He came to know that his brother and sister-in-law had ended their lives for his sake. He also ended his life and became a limestone. Bhanu became a tree bearing areca nut, his wife betel leaf and Veer provided lime. It made a tasty and digestive *paan*. Story sent a message, "The tall tree grew nuts called areca nuts. Creepers leaves were *paan* or betel leaves and from the limestone came lime paste that is added to preparation of *paan*. And this is how this loving family came together even after death. Together they taught people the values of love, unity and loyalty, and when people chew *paan*, they always remembered this story about them."

Payasam for a Bear is story of revenge that an animal took upon human couple. Mohan and Basanti promised a dish of *payasam* to a bear. They prepared it with gravel stones, dust, without sugar and sufficient milk. When the bear tasted it, he was quick to realize that he was cheated. He naturally got wild and punished the couple by putting their house on fire.

Fire on the Beard is a story about the pernicious result of laziness. Brij was a member of Idlers Club of the town. He was so lazy that he avoided getting up even when fire broke out in the town. It reached his beard. Half of his beard was burned down. At last he moved to escape from any further danger. It taught him the importance of activeness and alertness in life. "Finally Brij learned his lesson. Being lazy and pretending to be cool had certainly not helped him in his hour of need. So he shaved off his half burned beard, woke up early each morning and did all Shanti told him to do, nothing more!"

The Way You Look at It shows the importance of pluralistic approach in life. A stone lying in the river bed was viewed differently by different people. It was an image of Ganesh for Raju, where as it was an ideal piece for carving for a sculptor. A washer man thought it good for rubbing their clothes on it. For Ajit, it was a hurdle that must be removed immediately.

Roopa's Great Escape is about the importance of presence of mind in life. Bhalu kidnapped Roopa and took her to a remote place. She knew that she would not be able to overcome Bhalu in a straight fight. She intoxicated him, put him into a sack and informed the police. He was arrested and severely punished. "And that is what brave Roopa did. When she was in trouble, she did not talk to any stranger, but went straight to police for help. We must always remain cool like this when in trouble".

Five Spoons of Salt shows the ludicrous effect of lack of interactive communication between the members of a family. Gita's mother asked Gita to put five spoons of salt in *sambar*. Her grandmother knew of her forgetfulness. So she herself put five spoons of salt in *sambar*. Her grandfather, brother and sister also put five spoons of salt each. In fact Gita herself had put five spoons of salt. As a result *sambar* tasted only salty and nothing else. Had the members of the family communicated among themselves, there would not have been a mess like this.

How the Seasons Got their Share narrates the genesis of seasons. Day, Night, Summer, Winter, Rain and Wind were six brothers. God advised them to share the twenty four hours of a day and three sixty five days of a year within themselves. All started fighting. They decided to give three hundred and sixty five days to summer, winter, rain and wind. They soon realized that three hundred sixty five days season was unbearably long. So they divided a year in three parts- summer, rain and winter. Wind was allowed to blow for the whole year. Twenty four hours of a day were divided into night and day. Thus, the seasons came into existence.

The Island of Statue gives the message of environment awareness. Sculptor Amar had advised the King to prohibit the use of stones for sculpture. When the King's son Rajdip came to the throne, he allowed people to make statues out of the stones taken from the quarry. Very soon there were statues everywhere. There was continuous drought for many years after that. People fled the kingdom due to food shortage and water scarcity. Imbalance in natural resources hit the area and the people in the State.

The Kingdom of Fools shows how common people can be beguiled. Harish went to a betel leaf seller, purchased two hundred leaves and paid for it. Cleverly, he took only twenty five leaves and got a credit note for remaining hundred and seventy five. Then he went to a shawl merchant took a shawl for two hundred rupees, paid twenty five rupees to the shopkeeper and gave him a credit note which said "give hundred and seventy five". Shopkeeper thought that he would get hundred and seventy five rupees from the betel leaf seller. He failed to read between the lines properly. Harish succeeded in fooling the cloth merchant.

The Story of Silk is about the cleverness of a princess. Once a cocoon fell down from the mulberry tree into a hot water pot. The princess found that it contained silk. The king wanted to keep the secret of the silk. So he saw to it that the princess did not take cocoons with her after her marriage. But the princess was smarter than her father. She hid cocoons in her long hairdo. When she came to her groom's house, she continued to collect silk as before.

When Yama Called brings out the truth regarding the inevitable end of human being in death. Once Yama came to Arun's house. He treated him to gorgeous food, cool water and peaceful comfort. Yama was pleased with Arun and revealed his real identity to him. Yama promised him that he would intimate Arun of his death in advance. When Yama finally arrived to take him along to another world, Arun asked him about his promise. Yama told him that he had already warned him about his death through his white hair and falling hair. "A small smile appeared on Yama's lips. "But child, I did give you a warning. I made your hair turn white. I made your back stoop with age. I made your teeth fall out one by one. These were all indications that your time on earth has come to an end."

The Unending Story reveals the interminable nature of story telling. The King promised to give half his kingdom to a person who would tell him stories one after the other without stop. Many tried and failed. His smart minister however took up the gauntlet and started telling the same story of ant and sack of sugar in such a way that the King was bored. The minister said "There was an ant, she took a granule of sugar from a sack carried it to a safe place. She came back, took a grain of sugar, carried it to a safe place" He repeated the same thing so many times that the King was ready to give half his kingdom to stop his story.

After narrating every story the grandmother discusses it with the kids. And this is the part which brings the crux of every story they listened to. The visualizations of the kids and the lessons they learned are all discussed at last which further increases the curiosity of the reader to read all the stories covered in the book.

Though we miss this discussion in the later part of the book, yet the stories keep us excited and interested enough to read.

Ajji's stories are based on the values of courage, intelligence, foresight, and kindness. There are stories where she tells the significance of listening to others, how with the help of intelligent people in our life we can overcome any problems. The importance of being active in life, the goals that can be achieved through courage and determination, our outlook and perception of things and a lot of other emotions and values are discussed via engaging, interesting stories of different characters. The characters are so lively and imaginable that one starts connecting with them. There are stories about shopkeepers, mouse, kings, Gods, sculptors and other people.

The author has no doubt done a wonderful job of highlighting the importance of family bondings. In between the storytelling sessions, the family chores are very well inserted by the author. The concept of the grandmother telling a story a day is really nice as it keeps the stories length at a pace enough for young readers to carry on with their reading habit.

This book is truly one of the finest books of short stories. The language used in the book is simple and easy to understand with the inclusion of new words for kids to learn. Everyone will like this to be a part of kid's books library.

Through *Grandma's Bag of Stories*, Sudha Murty recreates the traditional way of storytelling, where kids sit around a grandparent, while getting mesmerised by one interesting tale after another.

As the book starts, the setting is that of summer, and a few children go on a holiday to their grandparents' home in Shiggaon, Karnataka. They proceed to do what children do best - find someone to play with. They befriend the kids next door, and have loads of fun with them. From taking a fun picnic to visiting the weekly market, they enjoy every minute of their vacation. But their favorite thing to do is listen to their grandmother's fantastic stories.

Grandma's Bag of Stories contains the stories that the grandmother narrates to entertain the seven young children. The tales are magical, and replete with captivating characters. Moral lessons are subtly blended in with the tales to impress the differences between what is right and what is wrong.The illustrations by Priya Kurian make the book more interesting and keep the young readers engrossed.

Most of the stories are being narrated by Ajji, but on few occasions, other village characters narrate these stories too.

There are 22 stories, and preceding those stories are glimpses of the children's lives and why the narrator told the story. All the chapters are named after the story. There are surprising, humorous, poignant and happy stories. There's a story where a bear wants to eat *payasam* (kheer), there's a story where a princess got turned into an onion, there's a story where a lazy man didn't put off a fire till it reached his beard, and many more such colourful stories. The writing style is witty and remarkable. There are pretty illustrations too.

Grandparents Bag of Stories

Grandparents' Bag of Stories by Sudha Murty is a follow up to her popular Grandma's Bag of Stories. Published during 2020, this tome contains relatable tales from the pandemic. The children in the tales stitch facemasks, help out with the cleaning, cooking and other chores of the house and even assist their family in helping those in need. In between the daily chores, they hear fascinating tales about kings and thieves, Gods and Goddesses, beanstalks and strange kingdoms from their grandparents.

Sudha Murty with her words, once again makes the readers fall in love with her writing. The stories that will entertain kids with lessons for life. Each story is beautifully narrated with a lesson for life.

There are many stories like a sibling story, Goddess of luck, Arrival of rice, the world of wheat and many other while we are unaware of. Especially the sibling story. Why Naga Panchami is celebrated is wonderfully explained by the author. I cannot choose any one story to be my favourite, each story is special to me.

Summary

Significantly it was 2020 and children were stuck indoors as the novel coronavirus (COVID-19) found its way into India. A nationwide lockdown is announced and amidst the growing crisis, Ajja and Ajji welcome their grandchildren and Kamlu Ajji into their house in Shiggaon. From stitching masks, sharing household chores, preparing food for workers to losing themselves in timeless tales, the lockdown turns into a memorable time for the children as they enter the enchanting world of goddesses, kings, princesses, serpents, magical beanstalks, thieves, kingdoms and palaces, among others. The myriad stories told by their grandparents become the biggest source of joy, making the children compassionate, worldly-wise and more resilient than ever. Following the trail of the best-selling *Grandma's Bag of Stories*, India's favourite author Sudha Murty brings to you this collection of immortal tales that she fondly created during the lockdown period for readers to seek comfort and find the magic in sharing and caring for others.

References

Bates, H. E. (1941), *The Modern Short Story: A Critical Survey*, Boston, The Writers' Incorporation. p. 15/16

Murty, Sudha (2004), *How I Taught My Grandmother to Read and Other Stories*, New Delhi, Penguin Books India, p. 07

Murty, Sudha (2006), *Magic Drum and Other Favourite Stories,* New Delhi, Penguin Books India, Preface.

Murty, Sudha (2012), *Grandma's Bag of Stories*, New Delhi, Penguin Books India, 2012.

9

How the Earth Got Its Beauty & The Serpent's Revenge: Unusual Tales from the Mahabharata

"We can give our children only two things in life which are essential. Strong roots and powerful wings. Then they may fly anywhere and live independently. Of all the luxuries in life, the greatest luxury is getting freedom of the right kind."- Sudha Murty

In fact, this is the latest title in Murty's chapter book series, after *How the Sea became Salty* and *How the Onion got its Layers*, this one too is sure to fire up the imagination of children and captivate them.

How the Earth Got Its Beauty

How the Earth got its Beauty dwells on the marvels of the natural world around us--think vast oceans, tall mountains, exotic animals – and encourages kids to think about how these wonders came into existence. The perfect blend of charm and simplicity, Murty's writing always engages young readers and teaches them many interesting things in a fun way. With beautiful illustrations and artwork, *How the Earth got its Beauty*, by Puffin, is another addition to her impressive repertoire.

Basically this is the story of a time when Mother Nature disguised herself as a ten-year-old girl and came to Earth. Then what happened and how Earth became so beautiful with lush greenery, colourful flowers, snow-capped mountains, and blue oceans is engagingly narrated in this book. The tale of how such beauty came into existence is a curious one indeed. India's favourite storyteller brings alive this timeless tale with her inimitable wit and simplicity. Filled with enchanting illustrations, this gorgeous chapter book is the ideal introduction for beginners to the world of Sudha Murty.

In her own words, " During my travels, I often see different landscapes – snow-clad mountains, meadows of flowers, singing rivers, animals of various shapes and sizes and the colourful life inside waterbodies. I became curious about the artist who has made this delightful chaos. Who is the magical painter who has created this incredible Earth?"

In this book, there's a girl. She tells everyone that her name is Devi, but her real identity has a little twist! She wanted to see if humans are doing well on earth and if they wanted anything more. She found three sisters who she felt have everything they needed to lead a happy life but the sisters said they were very bored with their lives. With a colourful and captivating cover and an intriguing blurb, this book is catchy and attracts readers both young and old. Then the story is simply yet engagingly told in such a way that young readers instantly connect with it.

To make their life of their own imagination, she gave them an opportunity. So, will the three sisters be able to make the most of that opportunity to make their life happier? Will the girl be able to make their lives interesting again? Read this book to find out how!

This book shows how the love and warmth of Mother Earth embraces everyone, while making sure that its beauty and serenity are not muddled and destroyed by people's desires and greed to own it. Nobody can own Mother Earth's creations like birds, animals, mountains, stars. In a bid to own more, we often forget to be grateful for what we already have and what nature has already blessed us with.

It also touches upon the vice that even a little bit of power makes us selfish and greedy.

This also reinstates that earth is our home and we need to care for it as much as it cares for us. We need to pledge together that we will not pollute air, water, land and protect its beauty the way it is.

The illustrations are vivid and beautiful. They make me want me to go out and enjoy the beauty of mountains, the serenity of rivers, the chirping of birds, and the greenery of trees.

The book is set in the decades following the creation of earth. Humans can be seen living in harmony, making use with the resources at hand. Mother Earth decides to find out if humans are indeed leading a good life and comes to a village in the disguise of a ten-year-old girl. As she meets three sisters, Sunaina, Shyama and Seeta, she realises that there are tremors of discontent in their souls—a longing for something different from their present realities. While one sister wants to see snow-capped mountains, another wants a big blue water body and fruits that tasted like nectar. The third wants to see animals, birds and insects in the most vibrant colours possible.

Is their wish fulfilled? As the story unfolds, one comes across consequences of letting arrogance and ambition take over ideas of greater good. It also shows the perils of counting one's chickens before they are hatched. There are several such ideas underlying the story, but at no point does Murty allow the book to get preachy. The message to kids is to always be compassionate towards nature. "Whenever humans become selfish and uncaring towards Mother Earth, she makes her presence felt and restores the balance in the world..." writes Murty. There couldn't be a wiser lesson, perhaps, at a time when the world is witnessing the perils of climate change.

In sum, a remarkable story narrated simply and endearingly for young readers.Have you ever stopped to marvel at the earth's beauty: at snow-capped mountains and oceans so deep; at colourful flowers and extraordinary animals? The tale of how such beauty came into existence is a curious one indeed. The chapter book series with Sudha Murty features a wonderful set of books that introduce magical stories to kids by India's favourite author. The series brings together timeless tales told in accessible language and supported by stunning full colour artworks that make these absolute keepsakes in a child's library.

Now we turn into her another interesting book, *The Serpent's Revenge.*

The Serpent's Revenge: Unusual Tales from the Mahabharata

It is pertinent to note that Hindu religious texts, scriptures and epics are rich repository of wisdom. These are much researched and annotated. With all the books on Hindu mythology and the epics, you would think there's nothing more to be written about. But Sudha Murty's latest book *The Serpent's Revenge: Unusual Tales from the Mahabharata* surprises you.

The Serpent's Revenge by Sudha Murty is the collection of selected few *Mahabharata* tales put together in the order. All the tales included in the book are timeless, unusual but not unheard. They are all seen, heard and read.

The one who are well versed with the stories of *Mahabharata* will have nothing new to read in the book. May be if the author has added her own reflection and analysis with each story it would have added some value to the book.

How many names does Arjuna have? Why was Yama cursed? What lesson did a little mongoose teach Yudhisthira? The Kurukshetra war, fought between the Kauravas and the Pandavas and which forced even the gods to take sides, may be well known, but there are innumerable stories set before, after and during the war that lend the *Mahabharata* its many varied shades and are largely unheard of. Award-winning author Sudha Murty reintroduces the fascinating world of India s greatest epic through the extraordinary tales in this collection, each of which is sure to fill you with a sense of wonder and bewilderment.

Now, the serpent's revenge is a unique collection of events from *Mahabharata,* some are known and some are unknown to me. This book will not only help you to narrate bed time stories for your kids but will also add to your knowledge about Indian mythology. There are many such stories which you have not heard from your parents or grandparents which are perfectly represented by the author with the help of striking pictures.

Many stories are provided with end notes or rather footnotes, where current location of India and stories behind it is being written by the author, which is the best source to know about that particular place and event and why we still worship and importance of that lord. Last two pages of the book depict the family tree of Chandravansh which is good source of information about Kaurava's and Pandava's.

All the stories were the mere narration. At the best they will refresh your memory about the tales. I almost forgot the eleven names of Arjuna but there is a chapter in the book on Arjuna's various names, their meaning and how he was conferred with those names. Also a tale of The Golden Mongoose was enlightening to read.

May be there is nothing new to read in this book but it is definitely a great well-written book with illustration to read out to your little budding readers at home. Yes it is a perfect book to introduce *Mahabharata* to the young readers making them acquainted with the epic. No doubt children were in the mind of Sudha Murty while writing the book as she has kept the language simple and easy to understand.

The *Mahabharata* is full of tales that people have forgotten simply because these days no one turns back to the original texts but relies on telefilm adaptations which usually focus on the more dramatic episodes.

Sudha Murty has chosen to retell stories which most people know but which are these days overlooked except perhaps for the story of Yudhisthira and the dog on the pathway to heaven. Readers – and this is certainly not a book just meant for children who might require explanations into the nature of Bhishma's celibacy for example – will find stories that illustrate the nature of *dharma* and the subtly balanced differences between the true way of life and the false.

Much of the *Mahabharata* is about behaviour and following the traditions of courtesy – which is why the serpent takes its revenge on Parikshit who insults a sleeping *sadhu* because he is overcome by thirst. Shankuntala too unwittingly breaks the laws of hospitality and is punished – and found a place in *Kalidasa* which gave her immortality as a literary heroine.

What is obvious is that punishment for rule breaking is swift and unexpected – though in Bhishma's case retribution is slow and involves transgender issues as the rejected princess Amba is reborn as Shikhandi whom Bhishma recognizes as a woman and will not fight.

Murty also reiterates the fact that Krishna while being an avatar of Vishnu has his own strategies which may or may not conform to generally received notions of good and evil – he encouraged his subjects to run away from a war, preferring commonsense over medieval honour, so that one of his names means 'Turncoat'. He also illustrates the fact that the divine 'big picture' is very different from human imagination.

Complexity is part and parcel of what Murthy narrates and there is a host of characters as might be expected from such a vast epic and twists and turns in relationships. The intervention of parents and grandmothers will certainly be required to explain the tales from time to time which may revive an ancient tradition of bonding now falling into disuse.

References

Murty, Sudha (2016), The Serpent's Revenge: Unusual Tales from the Mahabharata, Penguin Books India Pvt Ltd.

Murty, Sudha (2021), How the Earth Got Its Beauty, India Puffin.

10

The Daughter from a Wishing Tree

"Life is an exam where the syllabus is unknown and question papers are not set. Nor are there model answer papers."-Sudha Murty

At the outset, the women in Indian mythology might be fewer in number, but their stories of strength and mystery in the pages of ancient texts and epics are many. They slayed demons and protected their devotees fiercely. From Parvati to Ashokasundari, this collection features enchanting and fearless women who frequently led wars on behalf of gods, were the backbone of their families and makers of their own destinies.

The Daughter from a Wishing Tree by Sudha Murty is a simply yet vividly written collection of stories featuring moral based stories about women from Indian mythology. A perfect read not only for adults but also children, this is one book that all parents should buy and read to their kids and/or let them read it themselves.

The book published by Penguin India created quite a buzz amongst a section of bibliophiles, particularly those who love mythological stories.

"This is a mythology book - Women in mythology other than 'Sita and Draupadi. It will deal only with Hindu mythology," Murthy told PTI, giving a brief insight

Elaborating, she said: "It is very tough actually (to write such a book) because most of it is written by men, so very few women are there."

The Daughter from a Wishing Tree, is one of the books from the four-part series on Hindu myths by Sudha Murty. This book mainly focuses on the women in Hindu mythology and narrates the lore of their virtues. These women, though few have had important parts to play in these legends, often make decisions that have affected the entire course of events in the protagonist's story. Many of these women have paved their way in a man's world and written destinies with their own hands. The book goes on to unfold the tales of twenty-four such women who have had the power to influence fate itself – The bold Goddess of chaos, Kali; the serene Goddess of wisdom, Saraswati; the epitome of courage – Goddess Durga; the ethereal Goddess of beauty and wealth, Lakshmi; the sacred Ganga and Vatsala, the forgotten wife among others.

Outline

It is significant to note that the book is divided into four chapters with further divisions according to the legends. The chapters have Sanskrit names that vividly capture the essence of the stories that follow. Intricate illustrations by Priyankar Gupta accompany each fable and offer the reader a glimpse of another world.

In fact the cover story, *The Daughter from a Wishing Tree*, follows Goddess Parvati who, upon visiting the garden of Nandana at Amravati, the capital of Lord Indra's kingdom, makes a wish to Kalpavriksha, the Wishing Tree, asking for a daughter. *The Source of Knowledge* tells the reader about the creation of Saraswati, the Goddess of wisdom and knowledge, by Lord Brahma. *The Woman of the Battlefield* tells the reader how Goddess Durga comes to yield her eight characteristic weapons and goes on to slay Mahishasura, the *asura* who had wreaked havoc on the earth and subsequently, in the realm of the Gods. Other stories include, *The Maiden of The River, The Temple without a Deity, The God with The Head of a Horse,* and *The First Clone in The World,* etc.

A Critical Evaluation

In fact, the book is written in simple language which is no surprise considering the writer's slight aversion to dictionaries. This feature of the book not only makes it easily comprehensible by all but, also a must-read. Most of the books based on Hindu mythology in the market glorify the male legends and the role of women in these stories is often limited. This book gives the women in Hindu mythology the much-deserved limelight and presents their tales in a thought-provoking manner. It offers an insight into the world of Hindu mythology which is considered one of the oldest mythologies in the world and therefore, is perfect for individuals who have recently gained interest in the subject. Apart from mythology enthusiasts, psychology, anthropology, sociology, philosophy, and history lovers should also read this book as it discusses topics that would provide them with a better understanding of the Hindu religion, traditions, culture, psyche, polity, etc.

It is apt to mention here that *The Daughter from a Wishing Tree,* discusses morals and themes that are rarely talked about in the real world. Seeing women, who followers of Hinduism have known about since their childhood through folklore, being portrayed as the remarkable protagonists they are, makes them a source of inspiration even today.

Sudha Murty has done a wonderful job by sharing these unheard stories which proves that women are no less than men. I really admire this book as in a patriarchal society like ours, it can be the medium through which everyone can realise how powerful a woman is! Especially, when there seems no possible way to save the day.

The writing style of Sudha Murty is what all we all are familiar with. And it goes without saying that "She has done it again!" *The Daughter from a wishing Tree* is another masterpiece by her. It is no less than any of her past works. In fact, it just gets better and better!

"From Parvati to Ashokasundari, Shakti to Bhamati, you will encounter enchanting women who frequently provided assistance to the world and even the Gods in this book!", it read.

At the outset, a reading of *The Daughter From a Wishing Tree: Unusual Tales about Women in Mythology* obviously requires some level of suspension of disbelief, for, dear reader, you are about to enter the Harry Potter-esque world of talking objects, kings transfiguring into frogs, and dwarves and Goddesses descending on earth to flow as present rivers. Murty's book is obviously a mythological offering, so whether you're avowedly religious or staunchly atheistic, you can sit down to a reading guaranteeing yourself the pleasure of the stories.

Amidst the magic and the incantation, however, emerges the sage princess who created the first human clone in mythological history. Out of the mist of male disparagement, rises the goddess created by the Hindu Trinity (Brahma+Vishnu+Shiva) to slay *asuras* like a boss.

Shurpanakha's tale is particularly delightful to read, when you think of the manner in which most of us have probably grown up reading her. Shurpanakha was seen as a mere narrative ploy to bring Ram into the battle, a mere catalyst to a larger scheme of things that she is not party to, a woman devious and jealous of another woman's beauty apparently and a woman who 'rightfully' suffers the cutting down of her nose. This, at least in my memory of abridged and picture-heavy children's *Ramayanas*, was also always aggravated by depicting Shurpanakha as an ugly, often grey-complexioned *rakshasa* woman with a snout for a nose, and who deserved what was coming to her.

Here, however, refusing to be tethered by patriarchal expectations of the brave-BUT-generous, fierce-BUT-forgiving prototype of the female warrior, Shurpanakha of Lanka plots and schemes at her lowest moments to exact revenge for a broken heart.

Here's the deal: are all of the book's stories unequivocally about a woman? Absolutely. But do they unequivocally convey the badassery you expect entirely women-dominated warrior/magic/power stories to convey?

Not really. To be fair, Murty, perhaps, has the weight of a thousand years' worth of mythological stories – not to mention the weight of applying the lens of accuracy and verisimilitude to said stories – to blame for that.

While she has fused each of her chosen tales with characteristic charm and delightful dialogue – both authorial liberties – she chose not to accord the same liberties to the stories themselves. Which means, you could be rooting for Satyabhama all along, and empathise when she says things like: 'I can't believe my husband (Krishna) offered xyz flower to Rukmini (another wife) instead of me (also offering an undercurrent of resentment at the fact that her husband even has other wives apart from herself)', you resign yourself to the fact that ultimately, she'll be the one who's taught a lesson, because that, allegedly, is the crux of the tale that fits within other tales that fit within epics that people have read and believed in for years. Krishna has always had other wives in mythology, and his wives only have to get along – and so Satyabhama has to learn the art of "unconditional love, not possession," as a wily Narada chastises her.

Unfair, no?

That undercurrent of mutinous dissatisfaction with some of the women's arcs runs through a few of *Wishing Tree's* chosen twenty-four stories. The origin story of

Mandodari, for instance, is saddening; as a frog in a previous life, she asks for a boon from a group of sages, requesting that she be reborn a beautiful princess who marries an emperor. What's disappointing is that she asks for no powers for herself, ending up, as mythological chronology deems fit, the wife of Lanka's Ravana, eventually "suffering" for not having asked the sages for happiness. Why oh why, was she, who so easily could have been the architect of *asura* queendom, forced to play second fiddle to the battle of two men – one of whom was her own ill-fated, ten-headed husband?

There are, of course, rare glimpses of how women shone even in the original epics from which Murty chose her tales. For instance, there is the story of how goddess Parvati yearned for a daughter because she wanted a companion who would truly understand her heart. Murty's epilogue to that longing is sweet and simple: "...it shows Parvati's...profound belief and knowledge that a daughter is indeed rare and precious – a discovery that people continue to make even today."

There could be two ways of consuming Murty's chosen stories: as a first-time adult reader; or as a first-time adult reader that already knows how the stories end (told to one by judicious *desi* grandparents or read in fable and folklore). But here's the deal: if you encounter the stories in a third way, as if you were picking up these perspectives and point-of-views in your own childhood, then it all makes sense! If you were to read *Wishing Tree* to your child – or encouraging your child to read it – at an impressionable age, what they're essentially picking up are the female-centric aspects of the larger epics, of chapters rich and replete with strong women characters, women characters with actual dialogue (reams and reams of dialogue – could you imagine that in the epics?), queens with minds and battle strategies of their own… then you would be doing the next generation—and feminism—a great service.

Think of the minds that were shaped before we had the Murty-prototype epic to turn to: the minds that were fed stories passed down through the ages, from one generation to the next, of servile women and all-knowing men, of devoted wives and defiant Kings, of Gods who favoured the latter and ordered the former to fall in. Think of the relish with which these have been churned out and woven for the next line of children and grandchildren to listen to. Think, also, of the inadvertent power dynamics this inevitably led to: the belief that men must always sit at the table, the idea that women can be relegated to the background, the fact that, in marriages, decision-making, bread-winning, and ultimate-power-wielding is usurped often by our fathers and not our mothers, the unfortunate circumstance that so many sons, still, are favoured over the birth of a girl--a far, far cry from Parvati's own longing for Ashokasundari.

Perhaps *Wishing Tree* can help change things a bit. Perhaps literature, as food for the soul, will feed also a spirit of equity and equality. God knows it's time.

Reference

Murty, Sudha (2019), Daughter From A Wishing Tree, Penguin Random House India.

11

The Mother I Never Knew: Portrayal of Women Characters and Thematic Concern

"Mythology has largely been written by men and focusses *on men - on wars and men, who went to war. But, there are women who influence the decisions of men."- Sudha Murty*

Celebrated author, Sudha Murty's *The Mother I Never Knew: Two Novellas* is a poignant tale of two men, Venkatesh and Mukesh, as they set out on a journey to find out the mothers they never knew. Both men are happy and settled in their respective lives when they come across a shocking truth.

Introduction

Venkatesh's is a story of a man's pricking conscience for the wrong his father did to his mother and his restless search for her. Setu Madhav Rao marries Bhagirathi against his mother's wish. His mother Champakka loved money, silver, gold and diamond so much that she forced Setu Madhav Rao to leave Bhagirathi within two months of their marriage and remarry another girl. Champakka construed a plot according to which news was spread that Setu Madhav Rao and his mother were said to have died in a train accident between Bombay and Pune. This left Bhagirathi with a child in her womb and wilderness of lifelong widowhood through out the remaining years of her life.

Venkatesh had a well settled job in State Bank of India. His wife Shanta had been exceptionally resourceful in investments to reap rich dividends later. With the help of her parents she had made investments in movable and immovable properties in Bangalore. Venkatesh's parents and grandmother had died within a short span of three years after his marriage with Shanta. This had been a decisive blow to Venkatesh as it left him alone in the family to face his vibrant wife. His wife Shanta and son Ravi did not care much for him as they looked at him as a poor bank employee living on a meager income. The treatment tortured him but he could not think of leaving a job prematurely. He knew that it would worsen his condition in the family,

When Venkatesh realises he has a half-brother from his father's extramarital liaison, his world changes. He finds his step-mother out and is pained to see the pitiful condition she is living in. He must make amends for what his father has done but the question that haunts him deep within is if it is really possible to undo everything. Mukesh is in a similar state of agony when he comes to know that he was adopted as a kid. Pushed by impulse, he decides to find his biological mother. But the farther he goes, the more unclear the picture becomes. He must decide towards whom his true love and loyalty lies: the woman whom he called his mother all his life and who raised him or the woman who has given him birth.

The two men are bound by the same dilemma and the same complexity of emotions. and it is important for them to find their way back to bring stability in their lives. The core interest of the book is in exploring if it is really possible to come to terms with a reality as blaring and as deceiving as that of Venkatesh and Mukesh.

A Critical Appreciation

This is actually a book comprising of two unrelated stories, in both cases there is a quest for an unknown mother. The first story is how a person sets out to undo a certain wrongdoing by his own father. The second is about a young boy whose seeming blissful family life is shattered when he discovers that he is adopted and goes in search of his birth mother.

Actually both the novellas explore the emotional complexities of two men when they find out about the mothers they never knew they had. Both the stories relate to the complex situations and emotions that protagonist's face. Both have to take certain decisions which change their life.

The language and theme also relaxes the reader and lets him relish the beauty of Sudha Murty's writing. It is commendable for its simple writing and good content. In the plot Sudha Murty explores relationships in depth. The characters are what drives this book and adds spice and colour to the simple plot.

Here it is pertinent to note that *The Mother I Never Knew* has everything – selfish people, illegitimate children, foster parents as well as people who are still down-to-earth in spite of their riches.

The first story of the book draws a contrast between the living conditions and culture of the two families belonging to the two opposite sides of poverty-line. Though the second story feels a little melodramatic, the writing style and the simplicity of the language captures readers mind in full attention. This fictional novel talks about human relations. Both the stories, though based on completely different backgrounds, strike a similar chord of emotion in the readers. Both the stories deal with family values and discuss about the turn of situations when maintaining a steady relationship with the family can become too difficult.

It will be relevant here to have a description of the theme.

THEMES

The first important theme of the novella is the indelible impressions and imperishable place of mother in child's life. There are two prominently active mothers and quite a few ordinary mothers in the novella. Shankar's mother Bhagirathi alias Bhagavva is the central character of this novella. Though she did not appear repeatedly, the action of the novella moved around her only. That is why, the title of the novella is *The Mother I never Knew*.

Second important theme of the novella is diabolic effects of money madness on the traditional domestic and social structure in modern India. India had been famous for its well-knit family structure all over the world for centuries. Liberalization policy brought personal aspirations to the forefront. Freedom of thought and expression overrode the previous sense of duty towards society. Progress became a keyword of personal life. Sudha Murty found the seeds of writing in this atmosphere.

Characterisation

As already stated, Sudha Murty's novel *The Mother I Never Knew* comprises two novellas that explore quests by two men each searching for a mother he never knew he had. Here, in the proposed paper entitled, "A critical study of Women characters in Sudha Murty's - *The mother I never knew*" the first part has been analysed. Venkatesh, a bank manager, stumbles upon his lookalike one fine day. When he probes further, he discovers his father's hidden past, includes an abandoned wife and child. Venkatesh is determined to make amends to his impoverished stepmother- and taken steps to repay his father's debt. Sudha Murty introduced the female characters ' Champakka, Indiramma, Bhagirathi, Shanta and Gowri' in the first part.

Bhagavva (Bhagirathi)

Bhagavva appeared only once towards the end of the novella. Readers come to know about her role through flashback references mostly. Entire novella is woven around her personality. She was a victim of Indian concept of ideal womanhood. She was a prey to the social conspiracy which taught women to subjugate themselves without interrogation. People may salute her for her exemplary spirit of dedication and *pativratya*. Fact however remained that she was wronged by her own kith and kin.

Story of Bhagavva's wretched life began with her birth. Her parents drowned when she was a toddler. Her maternal uncle Gopal Kulkarni and his wife Kaveramma brought her up rather unwillingly. She was, "As the years passed, Bhagirathi grew up to be a very beautiful woman. She was fair and attractive and had long, black hair. Many women were jealous of her. Kaveramma did not send her out alone often because she was afraid that someone might take advantage of her."

Widowhood was thrust upon her within two months of her marriage with Setu Madhav Rao not because her husband really died but because the news of his death was maneuvered successfully. Social sanctions prohibited Bhagavva from trying to find out the reality of her husband's death. She had no other option but to believe the news as true. She must have cursed her fate thousand times without trying to know the authenticity of the news even once. Prima facie, it seemed that it was her mistake to blame herself for the misfortune, but the claws of the orthodox society were so tight that she had to keep utter silence in the matter. Though her parents were not mentioned more than once, it appeared that Bhagavva must have been ill treated by her parents as well. This automatically led to her physical and emotional impoverishment.

Bhagavva lived a life of seclusion in village Shurpali. "In the old days, the Brahmins of Shurpali were very orthodox and Bhagirathi—a teenage mother and a widow—was bound by customs and traditions. It was mandatory for her to shave her head to be considered purified, thus clearing her husband's path to heaven. Her long, shining black hair was cut and her head shaved. Bhagirathi was barely aware of what was happening to her. For a few weeks, she lived her life a day at a time." Condition of a widow in Indian society was worse than that of an animal.

Nobody liked her company. Nobody wanted to associate and invite her. She was unceremoniously disowned by her parents and friends. Her participation in social functions was shunned. She was prohibited from entry to sacred places like temple. She was made to give up nutritious food and comfortable beds so as to kill her carnal desires. Bhagavva went through all these hellish experiences throughout her life. When Venkatesh met her at Dharwad she was all lost and emaciated.

Sudha Murty's character Bhagirathi-- a teenage mother and a widow-- was bound by customs and traditions and thought that her husband is dead, which was not true, and shaved her head to be considered purified, thus clearing her husband's path to heaven. In the beginning she had no desire to live, decided not to stay in her village mainly due to the gossiping about her modesty. She is afraid that her life and that of her son's life would be worse than a dog's, if she stays in the village. Here Sudha Murty opined that "We cannot change the society and people. This has been going on since the ancient times. It's always a goat that is victimized and not a tiger".

Bhagirathi struggled a lot to overcome many difficulties to raise her son. She decided to leave the village and started working as cooking maid in many houses for meager salary for many years. Due to her hard work, she raised her son to became a primary school teacher and made him to lead a decent family life. Lorraine Toussaint a Trinidadian-American actress and producer says, "We all have a dark side. Most of us go through life avoiding direct confrontation with that aspect of ourselves, which I call the shadow self. There is a reason why it carries a great deal of energy".

Venkatesh

Venkatesh is one of the most unfortunate and pitiable characters of the novella. Though he was born of respectable parents, he had been deprived of his voice first by his grandmother and later by his own wife. His father Setu Madhav Rao and mother Indiaramma were monitored and regulated by his greedy and dominating grandmother, Champakka. He had to get married with Shanta because he was not given any other option. He was neither consulted nor could he express his feelings voluntarily on his own. Suryanarayanrao and his wife Savitamma impressed Champakka with their financial power and social status. The problems were compounded by the in-laws. They forced him to borrow and buy for pompous show of their prestigious wealth. Gradually, he withdrew from family affairs and was glad to be transferred to Hubli.

Venkatesh was respected and revered by his assistants in the bank because he helped everybody who asked for it. A bank clerk Geeta had a child whom she had to feed after every three hours. Manager Shankar allowed her to leave bank after lunch break and looked after her counter himself. Once cashier Mahesh found excess amount of one thousand rupees which he and his friends wanted to spend on merry making. Venkatesh gave the money to the bank watchman for his wife's C section. "Everybody wanted to celebrate and have a party with the money, but Venkatesh disagreed, "No, that's not right. Let's keep it aside. We'll return it if the owner comes looking for it." When nobody came to claim the money, it was given to the office watchman Karim for his wife's C-section operation." This showed that he always had sympathy for weak section of society. It compensated for his distance from his own people.

Revelation that he had a twin in the surrounding area changed the course of his life for him. His past slid before his mind's eye. Human element in him did not let him sit still and comfortable. He found out his stepmother and stepbrother. He took upon himself to rectify the mistake made by his father by planning to assist her with fifty lakh rupees. He told his son, "You are right, we are not responsible at all, but when I inherited my father's property I also inherited his share of mistakes. Appa failed in his duties towards them. We can't undo the past, but may be we can make their life little easier, especially since we have so much of wealth".

Champakka

Venkatesh's grand mother, Champakka, a loud mouthed old widow, lived solely for the sake of her son, faced a tough life to raise her son. She protected her son from all the problems and happily ruled the whole family, but sometimes dominated the family members.

Indiramma

On the other hand, Venkatesh's mother, Indiramma, portrayed as quite, innocent and submissive. She passes her time, by knitting, embroidering painting and indulging herself in order to avoid any confrontations with others. The work of Betty Friedan, *The Feminine Mystique,* is the main source of information on the condition of these housewives. She defines house wife as: The home maker, the nurturer, the creator of children's environment is the constant recreator of culture, civilization and virtue.

Gauri

Gauri--Venkatesh's daughter, was quiet and intelligent girl and also an eternal optimist. She could make anyone feel better. Venkatesh always loved her because of her intelligence, calm and ability to remain silent in any situation that brings success and peace to her life. She always spent very good time and frank discussion with her father. She always follows her conscience. In one occasion when her father undergoes a tough situation to pay his father's debt, she decided to give forty five lakh from her account, which was invested in a fixed deposit by her mother in her name to avoid income tax, or may be for her marriage and thus saved her father from a major problem.

Here, Sudha Murty tries to explain that today's generation is much wiser. A good narration between father and daughter from the book: Her father asked her, 'Gauri, your mother will find out about this. You know that. What will you do then? She replied, 'I have not stolen this money

Anna, nor have I given it away to a cause that I don't believe in. I am not afraid of her or anyone else. No matter what people say, I'll always follow my conscience.' Venkatesh asked, 'Why did you do this Gauri?'. She replied, 'That's so easy Anna. You want to pay back a debt that your father owes somebody. I want to pay back a debt that my father owes too'

Shanta

Venkatesh's wife, Shanta, ran the house very efficiently, handled the family finances better than an investment banker. She is always conscious of her appearances and proud to be a lady's club president. Active investor of the stock market because of her sound knowledge in business, she always speaks to the point.

Shanta played an enormous role in handling the lives of her husband, son and daughter. She loved herself so much that she never thought about her husband or daughter. She ill treated her mother-in-law and looked down upon her husband's middle-class status. She was pampered by her parents right from her childhood. The writer described her as, "Shanta grew up like a princess with her parents fulfilling all her demands. Her studies progressed and the family was transferred to bigger towns and cities until they finally ended up in Bangalore, where Shanta graduated with a bachelor of Arts from Maharani's College."

Shanta was blinded by her family richness. She was the only daughter of her parents and naturally the sole legal heir to their property. Fortunately for her, her mother-in-law, father-in-law and grandmother-in-law died within a short span of three years after her marriage. That brought her an absolute authority to have her own way in family matters. She and her father Suryanarayanrao took all the decisions related to Venkatesh's family. It increased her arrogance. She earned name and fame within a short time which made her autocratic by nature.

Shanta envied her prospective daughter-in-law and her own daughter. She was afraid that Pinki would snatch away her son, Ravi from her as she herself had severed her husband from his mother. She thought. "For a moment, Shanta envied Pinki, "Everything that I have struggled to earn will go to my daughter-in-law one day. My darling son Ravi will also belong to that girl. Maybe I should share my concerns with Venkatesh. Or may be I shouldn't. He won't understand anyway."

She was good only to those persons who consulted and listened to her. Ravi was a 'mom's boy'. He telephoned her from the USA but rarely talked to Gauri or Venkatesh because she had enslaved him. Gauri was different. She pursued her MBBS and specialized in Gynecology against Shanta"s wish. Shanta wanted her to do MBA and earn lakhs in short period. Thus we find that she had a personality clash with everybody who did not fall to her whims. Shanta treated her husband with scant respect and dispassionate emotions. Venkatesh had been smart enough to mind his own business without making any fuss on her behavior or trends of egoistic nature.

Here Sudha Murty described the nature of a modern girl and her perception towards her vision of family life. Through the characters Shanta and Gowri, it shows the sophisticated, business background, status of family members. They live their life for earning more and more money and no intimacy between the family members, indicating the modern false lifestyle. The novel also showcases individualities of the modern women's rights by describing an independent, skilled and gifted female protagonists like Shanta and Gauri.

In a nutshell, a woman is usually meek and humble that's the reason many of our women suffered a lot. They quietly bowed down and accepted injustices heaped upon them by men and fate. Sudha Murthy had not only written stories for children but she has also exposed the patriarchal control in our country and the tolerance of women in ignorance through her novels. To quote from Simone de Beauvoir's book titled *The Second Sex* wherein she asserts that: "Once she ceases to be a parasite, the system based on her dependence crumble, between her and the universe there is no longer any need for a masculine mediator". In all her novels, she shows a survival path to the female protogonist's that women can lead a successful life with sincere and hard work, without the help of those who ill treated them.

Now we will describe the thematic concern in *The Mother I Never Knew*.

Thematic Concern in Perspective

It is apt to mention first that objective work *The mother I never knew* of Sudha Murty comprises two novellas and explores quest by two men —each searching for a mother they never knew they had. The novel runs backward and forward extravagantly. It also arouses expectations about the future course of events. The reciprocal relationship of indecisiveness and amazement is a principal source of the charismatic power and liveliness of an ongoing plot. It's more prudent in its gist and manner. In the first novella injustice is done to Bhagiratti (Bhaggava) by her own husband and mother-in-law. She became a destitute courtesy her own people who also made her to live as a widow and his son as an orphan. Her stepson Venkatesh a bank manager didn't know about his other mother and started to search his father's past. Sudha Murty dives deep into the hearts of the people and digs out their behaviours, faults and agonies in these two stories.

Murty emphasizes the pleasant ambience in front of the readers, she focuses on the type of food eaten by the Karnataka people, the various places of Karnataka and how people address one another like amma, avva and anna. Rural life is juxtaposed in the novel. The novelist aroused curiosity in Venkatesh to meet his stepbrother Shankar and to know about him. He brings the oasis in the desert like life of Bhaggava. Murthy makes her character to actively participate in celebrations such as Ganesh Chaturthi, Dussehra, Kannada Rajyotsava and Ugadi by giving full enjoyment to her characters and brings out the importance of Indian culture and festivals in the novel.

The novelist also makes us familiar with the thread ceremony at Shiggoan and the food eaten by Venkatesh on the Banana leaf. The various types of food such as Chakkali, Avalakki and Besan laddu is described to bring taste to the mouth of the readers. Bakula flowers and Elaichi bananas in Yellapura and the Marikamba Temple in Sirsi are also described to bring the beauty to the Karnataka State. It represents an aspect of novelist experience of her place. The names of Indian rivers are also exposed in the novel.

Sudha Murty once interacted with the audience at Bangalore at Page Turners recently opened bookstore on MG road mentioned:

"Be honest, original and tell the truth, Real-life experience, true to the core, makes interesting reading, be it non-fiction or even while writing a novel"..

Obviously, she is an honest author and is always true to the subject at hand. Respect for mother is also realistically expressed by Murty by allowing Venkatesh to visit her stepmother Bhaggava with some fruits. Murty sees Bhaggava as a strong, old Brahmin widow, thin, with a torn white sari with a clean shaven head who seemed burdened with poverty. Bhaggava, an orphan child, was devoid of her parental, social, and economical love and suffered a tough life. She was beautiful in her youth with fair colour and long black hair and studied till fourth grade. While staying with her maternal uncle Gopal in Shurpali, she was married to her neighbour's distant relative Setu who was a cook in mutt in Matunga and was studying in Mumbai. Setu (Venkatesh's father) was young, intelligent and very handsome. After marriage Setu's mother asked him to stay in Mumbai for the exams.

After some days Bhaggava became pregnant, Bhaggava's mother- in- law came to perform *seemanthan* and was heard rumours that Bhaggava was in contact with

Hanuma (Gopal Uncle's son) and the child which she bears is not of her son Setu. She interfered in the marital life of his son by giving a wrong message and orders him to abandon her on the claim of infidelity. Setu her husband deserted her, and later she was told that her husband died in a train accident.

Obviously marriage is a best relationship, but the marital breakdown is more dangerous. Sudha Murty explains the deplorable seriousness in Bhaggava's life. She portrays that Bhaggava was shunned as a curse to the family. She was referred to as unlucky and shrewd - as she killed her parents at the time of birth and now she killed her husband. She was also avoided as a plague. She accepted the challenges and became invisible. Bhaggava never asserted for her rights, her condition was same as Virmati in *Difficult Daughters* of Manju Kapur. She was in the hands of the fate. As it is rumoured that women are women's worst enemy. She suffered antagonist behaviour, went through the trauma of allegations, indignity. She was blamed with baseless rumours and her own mother- in- law played dirty politics with her as she wanted to marry her son to someone offering more dowry. She spends her life with heavy burden of responsibility, lived as a widow though her husband was alive. It was sheer injustice done by her husband though she was virgin and pure and sacred.

Murty framed Bhaggava as a widow and she had to face many societal taboos and also suffered from financial stringency. She was saved by Chouda and she further left the village. She started to live in Dharwad and worked in houses like a maid to make both ends meet. She thought her husband dead and performed shraddha always on his death anniversary. She bathed newborns, took care of their mothers and cooked for people. Her hands became rough and she toughened up. Her son Shankar was a debilitated victim of childhood negligence by his father. Bhaggava's strength was Shankar; she made him to stand on his feet by making him a primary school teacher and on account of his job he was transferred to many places and later married a nice girl. Bhaggava suffered her entire life.

The story exhibits that Bhaggava's son Shankar suffered a poor man's life; he had no land and his daughter Mandakini used to take tuitions. On the other hand, contrary to it Murty disposes the beauty of Venkatesh family's beautiful home which was named as Anandita, which contains four bedrooms with attached toilets, teakwood doors, ultra modern facilities and separate quarters. In the novel the novelist has given all priorities and luxurious life to Venkatesh and on the other side made Shankar suffer whose father was also same but her mother was deserted and had to undergo only sufferance.

The novel discloses that Setu was the same person Venkatesh's father Madhav Rao who has changed his name from Setu Madhav Rao to Setu. He had missed the train and that train met with an accident and it was a second chance of life to him. He had committed a sin by deserting his wife and to compensate it he sends money order to her but she doesn't receive it as she had left for Shirupali. Setu was a mamma's boy, he was wrong on many levels, he listened to his mother and had discarded his wife and married another woman for money. The present novel is not only a subjective picture of wife desertion but it also emphasizes that one must not believe on other without properly investigating the real conditions.

The other story is of Mukesh. The second novella portrays the journey of Mukesh from one mother to other. He was born to an ignorant teenage mother Nirmala Kumari, and he was adopted by Rupinder and lastly he was brought up by Sumati. Sudha Murty had painted Nirmala as a teenage mother who is a tenth class student, a Zamindar's only daughter who was brought up with much care and protection, but commits a mistake which leads her to become pregnant. His father Zamindar wanted to marry his daughter into an influential family. She gets into a relationship with Anand who was living in the outskirts of her home. The poor, handsome young college student from a different community, to supplement his college education, was teaching Nirmala English. When he was injured, Nirmala tended to him. Love blossomed and they crossed all boundaries. She becomes pregnant. Thomas R. Murray mentions that: ―Some Critics of unwed teenage girls bearing children have charged that such behaviour is an outcome of irrational decision making in which girls fail to analyze the consequences of their act.‖7.(Thomas,R.M. 2009).

To maintain the honour of the family, Nirmala was kept away at her father's farmhouse far away from her own family to deliver the baby and to agree to remarry afterwards. She followed her strict father's advice. She was told to drop the baby on the temple stairs after the delivery and to maintain secret. It was a difficult job for Nirmala as a mother to discard her own baby. Her lover did not know of her pregnancy.

The novel depicts that Rupinder, a childless mother was a hard working Punjabi girl, who approached Nirmala and became friendly with her and came to know about the secret of pregnancy. Rupinder comes in the form of a saviour who was more potent than the destroyer. She was from border of Punjab and Haryana and was married to Surinder who was a school dropout and short-tempered man. As Rupinder had lost her child, she insisted Nirmala that she will take care of her baby. There is specific focus on the motherly love in Rupinder for want of a child. Her parents and brother were labourers in the Zamindar's house. Nirmala delivered a healthy baby boy and gave a golden chain to Rupinder and told her to give her baby this chain afterwards. Nirmala before handling the baby boy to Dulari had touched the baby's feet and uttered: — "Beta, please forgive me. I didn't know how a child was born and I brought you into this world in my ignorance. I don't know what your future holds, but I can't just leave you somewhere to die of hunger or cold. Rupinder is a nice woman. At the very least, she'll ensure your survival and you won't grow up as an illegitimate child. I pray to God that no woman gets punished the way that I'm getting punished now."

Amazingly, the very astonishing scene is that Dulari had dropped the baby on the temple stairs and it was picked up by Rupinder. The novelist explains that a crowd gathered around the baby and Rupinder insisted that her baby died one month before and she was ready to take care of the baby if no one claimed him. She took the baby to Jalna in Maharashtra to her in-laws place. Her husband's family and husband became unhappy with an Orphan with a dark patch. Her husband also persuaded her to drop the baby in Orphanage or leave him in Gurudwara. It signifies that people don't want other's baby, as they are selfish and never consider other's feelings and emotions. The love and desire to have a baby was only Rupinder, not her family. She gets hurt by the indifferent behaviour of her family.

(Mukesh) Munna had a dark patch on his right foot and it was considered by his grandmother as a bad omen. He was ignored, rejected by Surinder's family and also didn't receive love and family bonding and so he was forced to stay at Sumati's house. Rupinder's family decided to shift to Amritsar, but they didn't want Munna to be with them. It was considered that Munna will bring bad luck to them.

Sumati planned to take the photo of Neeru and Munna at the time of departure as a token of love. Rupinder suggested Sumati to adopt Munna and she agreed. Rupinder conjectures: Give him a good education and raise him to be a good human being. Knowing you, I'm sure that you will do that anyway.' Though she was crying, Rupinder felt a sense of satisfaction and relief knowing that Munna would have a good future. Rupinder desperately uttered that due to the way he was treated at her home by a bad mother-in-law and an alcoholic husband and a bickering family, he was better off with Sumati. Sumati and Rupinder were friends. Whoever the mother is, love for their child is a prority and all a mother wants is that he should be safe.

Interstingly the novel expedited the journey of Munna further, Munna or Mukesh approached Sumati's family and Rupinder introduced him as his son. Rupinder and Munna often visited Sumati's house. Sumati and her husband Krishna loved Munna which makes Rupinder happy. Sumati cared him and loved him as her own son. She encouraged and supported him in every phase of life. As the society and the family will look at him with different eyes, they didn't tell Munna that he was adopted. She informed her in-laws that she was pregnant and later on delivered a boy. Munna had brought luck to their family and day by day they became rich. Sumati's stitching business grew exponentially with each passing year. The family expanded the business with a new factory in Bangalore and stayed there. Later Munna became sad and disturbed when he it was revealed to him that he was an adopted child.

Summing it up, Sudha Murty manifested that no one supports a woman's delinquencies. She also highlights how human relationships change according to the conditions and how a woman feels alienated in male-dominated society. In the novel Sudha Murty exhibits the different roles played by different mothers. Bhaggava, Nirmala Kumari, Rupinder and Sumati are not only great women but they are fantastic and adorable mothers who are oppressed and are not given their rights in the male-dominated society. Sudha Murty had exposed through her artistic perception and innovative vision the invisible faults of the society permeating our culture, colluded by the power. This novel is of deception and injustice done by the patriarchal world. Life was not easy to all the mothers exposed in the novel. The novel is cool, the paras written are short and overall the female characters were dominated and unjustified by the male characters.

References

Beavour, Simone de (1952/ 1993), *The Second Sex,* New York: Alfred A. Knopf.

Frieden, Betty (1971), *The Feminine Mystique,* Harmondsworth: Penguin.

Murty, Sudha (2008), *Gently Falls Bakula,* New Delhi: Penguin Books.

Murty, Sudha (2014), *The Mother I Never Knew*: Penguin Books.

Prajapati, R.A. & Dr. Chaturvedi, Roopesh (2015), *Indian English Novelists: Critical Responses,* Allahabad: Takhtotaaz Publishers, p. 77.

Rafluddin, S.J. (2015), "Thematic concern of Sudha Murthy's novel the mother I never knew", *IOSR-JHSS,* Vol 20(10) pp 72-76 October.

Sanderson, D. Dwight. (2013), *Rural Sociology and Social organization.*LLC: Literary Licensing.p.11

Siddiqui, J.R.&Parab,V.V. (2015), *Human Relationships in Shobhaa De's Novels,* Chennai: Notion Press, p.197.

Silas, Baruch (2010), *The Irony of Love, Premarital and Extramarital Relationships*.

Thomas, R.M. (2009), *Sex and the American Teenager, Seeing through the Myths and confronting the Issues*, USA: Rowman and Littlefield Education, p. 134.

12

The Day I Stopped Drinking

Milk

"Money is one thing which rarely unites and mostly divides people."- Sudha Murty

Sudha Murty's *The Day I Stopped Drinking Milk* (Life Stories Here and There) is a collection of twenty-three real life stories delighting the readers of all ages. Over the years, Sudha Murty has come across some fascinating characters in real life whose lives made an indelible impression upon her mind and compelled her to write interesting stories about them because all these female protagonists had astonishing lessons to reveal. This is really great book that describes down to detail about how myriad characters, circumstances and events have had a prominent effect on the author's life. The best touch to this collection is that these are true life stories and we know that good people still walk this earth. Author writes about life, observations and experiences and that makes these little gems of stories more enjoyable. She works towards the betterment of the society and rural development.

In fact, the book is a recollection of her experiences. She has met several people whom we would normally consider inconsequential but Sudha Murty has lessons to learn from them all reminding us of the oft quoted line from Shakespeare 'sermons in stone and running brooks'.

She is intellectually honest. There is no touch of hypocrisy or cant about her and she can be a nice model for all aspiring young writers. She was asked whether she took permission of the characters whom she writes about. She answered that she has, for the people don't want their mistakes to be repeated by others. Of all virtues she commended the virtue of compassion. Sudha Murty has this virtue in abundance, as her stories will exemplify.

Published by the Penguin Books India, the last story in this slender volume is titled *Life's Secret Lessons*. This is quite significant. The first lesson that she learnt was that children speak the truth while adults have a befogged mind.The second lesson she learnt was during her travels to distant corners of India to witness the ravages caused by natural catastrophes or disasters. She realized the limitation of human power and though men have money power it can never be a substitute for life.

Sudha Murty does not hesitate to learn from her own son, Rohan, who taught her never to over-estimate herself. The last lesson that she learnt was when she was in Cape Town in South Africa, from a cab-driver who called Mahatma Gandhi a world leader. Though South Africa has produced outstanding men, people like the Buddha, Mahatma Gandhi, Martin Luther King Jr or Abraham Lincoln are compassionate leaders and belong to the entire humanity.

The Day I Stopped Drinking Milk which is the title of the book is about her visit to Odisha, more specifically about the poor tribals there. On the day she visited, there was sudden rain, which made it inevitable for her to take shelter in a hut. The owner's baby was crying as though it was playing *jugalbhandhi* with the platter of rains outside. The man of the house wanted her to have something to eat or drink. His wife was reluctant as she explained to her husband the difficulty of getting milk.

Sudha Murty overheard the conversation and felt ashamed of snatching the share of the milk meant for the baby. She first declined but on being repeatedly requested by the man of the house she finally agreed to take some milk. But in the process she learnt of the plight of the villagers and from that day onwards she stopped drinking milk.

A compassionate woman, modest to the core and unassuming by nature, Sudha Murty's book is interesting. Her readiness to learn is impressive and a true reflection of her personality. She reaches the height of simplicity. 'Simple living and high thinking' are no more with us bemoans Wordsworth in a sonnet but Sudha Murty is quite the contrary.Many people cannot express what they feel or think but in giving succinct expression to their thoughts, Sudha Murty reminds us of the line of Alexander Pope 'What oft was thought but never well so expressed.'

Female Protagonists in the Selected Stories

Remarkably, in the opening story, *Bombay to Banglore*, Sudha Murty was boarding Udyan Express at Gulbarga railway station as her destination was Bangalore. The ticket collector asked the thirteen-years-old thin, dark and scared girl who was hiding under Sudha Murty's berth to show her ticket. The girl did not say anything and stood quietly. Ticket Collector caught hold of her arms and told her to get down at the next station and he started forcibly pulling her out from the compartment. The travellers around the girl were not bothered at all and went about their business. Suddenly Sudha Murty had a strange feeling.

She stood up and called the T.C. "Sir, I will pay for her ticket. It is getting dark. I do not want a young girl on the platform at this time." T.C. asked her to pay from Bombay to Bangalore Sudha Murty paid it. As the train approached Bangalore, the girl started talking. Her name was Chitra and she lived in a village near Bidar. Her father was a coolie and she lost her mother at birth and father remarried. But a few months ago, her father died. Her stepmother started beating her often and did not give her food. She was tired of that life. So she left home in search of something better. Sudha Murty admitted Chitra in the shelter home and High School where she scored 85 percent in tenth. Then she did her diploma in Computer Science. She got a job in a software company. She was lucky because after some years her company was sending her to the USA!

Eventually Sudha Murty was invited to deliver a lecture in San Francisco. After the lecture she planned to leave for the airport. She went to the reception counter to pay the bill but the receptionist said, 'Ma'am you don't need to pay us anything. The lady over there has already settled your bill'. Sudha Murty turned around and found Chitra there. She asked Chitra, 'Why did you pay my hotel bill?'

With tears in her eyes and gratitude on her face she said, 'Akka, if you had not helped me, I don't know where I would have been today -- may be a beggar, a prostitute, a runaway child, a servant in someone's house… or I may even have committed suicide. You changed my life. I am ever grateful to you.' Then suddenly Chitra hugged me and said that she paid it because I paid for her ticket from Bombay to Bangalore!

Notably the story explains how Chitra's life was completely transformed after meeting Sudha Murty during a train journey from Bombay to Bangalore. Chitra had gotten onto the train without a ticket, but the author took her in and provided her with shelter. She studies and later moves abroad and is very appreciative of Sudha Murty's gesture. The most determined, dedicated and inspired girl -- Chitra confident and powerful -- the "protagonist" made her life from her predicament with her benefactor Sudha Murty. According to Anthony Robbins, "Power is the ability to produce the results you desire most and create value for others in the process. Power is the ability to change your life: to shape your perceptions, to make things work for you and not against you."

Rahman's Avva is the second story. Kashibai is the protagonist. Fatima Bi was her neighbor. However, both of them did not see eye to eye at all. It is not that they were bad women but their nature was very different. Kashibai was loud, frank and hardworking. Fatima Bi was quiet, lazy and an introvert. Inevitably, there was a fight. But when Kashibai heard that Fatima was admitted to the hospital in critical condition and delivered a son, she started crying forgetting her enmity. They also learnt the next day that Fatima Bi was no more. One night the child started crying non-stop. Her motherly instinct made her go next door. She picked up the baby, held him in her *pallu* and brought him to her house holding him tightly to her chest. The body named Rahman grew up in Kashibai's house and started calling her Avva. When Rahman's father died of tuberculosis Rahman was left alone. Kashibai was conscious about his religion. Every Friday she sent him for *namaz*. She told him to participate in all Muslim Festivals. Kashibai's affection and devotion overwhelmed Rahman. He prayed to Allah and then touched Kashibai's feet. He said, "Avva, you are my Ammi. You are my Mecca." This is a heartwarming story of the life of a Muslim named Rahman, who was brought up by his Hindu neighbor. In simple language the story moves the hearts of the readers and we realize how blessed we are. Uneducated but far advanced in human values, Kashibai the – protagonist -- had raised Rahman with his own religion and still loved him like her son.

The third story is *Ganga's Ghat*, where the female protagonist -- Ganga, a coolie in a small village gets up in the morning, goes to the field to work, earns her daily wage and then comes back in the evening, fetches water, bathes, cooks her meal, eats and sleeps to get up in the morning. It is her routine. It was very hand to get water in the summer because there was no electricity. Summer was a curse to the village.

One summer evening, she came back after work and felt very tired. She started cooking when she saw an old beggar in front of her hut. Ganga said, "old man, I haven't cooked yet and I have very little rice today. You can come another day and I will give you some food." Then he said, "Akka, I do not want rice. Can you give me one bucket of lukewarm water? My body is itchy. Someone said that I should take a bath in lukewarm water. That will reduce the itching. I am unable to sleep at night. In the summer, there is a lot of dust and it is affecting me in this old age."

At this, Ganga was upset as it was not easy to get water from half kilometre away. But the beggar requested her and convinced her that she had a hut, vessels, firewood and water. Ganga had an indescribable feeling as nobody had told her that she was rich. Nobody ever called her Akka. This was an unusual feeling and she liked it. She gave him a bucket of lukewarm water daily and the number of beggars for bath increased day by day. The word had spread. People knew that if you want to have a bath you should go to Ganga's Ghat. We are introduced here to an old lady, who desires to achieve something in life. She experiences contentment as a result of seeing to the needs of her fellow villagers by setting up a bathing facility.

Ganga had found her mission in life. She never got public recognition. She said that it gave her an opportunity to serve people who don't have anything in life. Sudha Murty met Ganga for her service she was offering to the beggars and needy people and said, 'Ganga, I will give you a box of soaps and a hundred cotton towels.' But Ganga explained to Sudha Murty that she wanted to do the work within her own limits. Money comes with expectations and spoils the delicate equilibrium of social work. Ganga -- the protagonist's, bathing ghat was no less than Ganga's ghat at Varanasi, Hardwar and Rishikesh as she provides provides bathing water to hundreds of people in a drought stricken area.

The Day I Stopped Drinking Milk is the next story of Sudha Murty dealing with a woman in a flooded village in Odisha which teaches Sudha Murty a life lesson she will never forget. In the coverstory, we are introduced to a family residing in Odisha, with whom the author had once stayed during her visit to the village. As the author is the guest to the family, host wished to give her some food or drink. The author asked for a glass of milk at which they were completely unable to meet her request. Sudha Murty was working in a remote village. They were building a school for children in a beautiful surrounding of mountain, lake and greenery. Suddenly it started raining heavily. So her translator knowing Oriya and English suggested to take shelter in the nearest hut. The hut was small and had thatched roof and mud flooring. The host came and welcomed them. The owner's baby was crying inside and his mother was singing a lullaby to soothe him. After sometime, the translator got bored and went to a shop near the hut. The host wanted to give her something to eat or drink. The Taittiriya Upanishad says, *Athiti devo bhava*. He offered her tea but she denied as she never drank tea or coffee. After some time he asked her is she would drink milk. Sudha Murty did not want to hurt his feelings by denying everything. So she nodded her head in affirmation. Her host thought that she did not understand Oriya because she had a translator. But she knew Oriya, though she was not able to speak it fluently. Hearing her husband the wife was very upset. She said in an irritated tone, "The lady sitting outside has grey hair but no common sense. We are poor people. We also have to take care of a child. I have only one glass of goat's milk. I have to work hard even to get this milk. If madam wants tea, I can give her a few teaspoons of milk. If she wants to eat fish, I can fetch them from the pond and prepare and excellent fish curry. If she wants to it *pakhala*, it is already there. But she should not ask for an expensive drink such as milk."

Helping the dead is about a group of young people who form a voluntary organization to help poor people who have nobody to cremate of bury their dead ones. *Three ponds* is about the sacrifices of three different women for providing water to others. *No man's garden* is about a rich farmer growing vegetables in a wasteland for the poor and needy. *Sticky bottoms* is about her friend whose only concern is talking about himself. ***Too many questions*** is about how the managers try to come in between the donor and the receiver. ***Gift of sacrifice*** is about a young cowherd who sacrifices his life for his village while giving the message from a soldier to the captain. ***Bad Help*** is about how helping somebody may be a life-long burden for him to carry. ***Sharing with a ghost*** is about a young man who learns from a ghost that "in life sharing is important".

Foot in the mouth is about people who gossip and how they find people to gossip about. In ***Miserable success***, we realize that being successful doe not necessarily mean being happy. In ***Shraddha***, we realize that in the eyes of God, girls and boys, sons and daughters are equal. In ***Lazy Portado***, we learn that as a student, we should study, get knowledge, learn skills and work hard. ***Uncle Sam*** is about a person who regrets going to America. *You should have asked me* is about how people want their egos to be fed. *A mother's love* is about how a mother climbs a hill and jumps down in order to be with her baby. *Do you remember* tells us that we remember all that we consider as important.

The last story in the book is *Life's Secret Lessons* wherein the author learns seven lessons in life.

First lesson: Only children tell the truth and are real judges of one's talent.

Second lesson: You cannot substitute many things in life with money.

Third Lesson: Wherever there is money, people like to take advantage of the situation and maximize their return.

Fourth lesson: If we keep collecting material things, it becomes a burden to the next generation.

Fifth lesson: To be patient and to recognize people's intentions.

Sixth lesson: We must stand up for ourselves and follow our heart, even if other people do not always agree with us or like it.

Seventh lesson: We should not hear other sounds and can concentrate on what we are doing.

Eighth lesson: When a person becomes a compassionate leader, they do not belong to one country.

In Sudha Murty's ignorance and on host's insistence, she had agreed to drink milk but she was not even aware that she was snatching the share of a little baby. She felt ashamed. When translator returned, she told him to tell the host that she was on fast. The translator was baffled because he had seen her having milk in the morning breakfast. The host asked,

'Nobody fasts on Wednesday. Why are you fasting today? She said, 'I fast on Wednesday for Buddha'. From that day onward, Sudha Murty stopped drinking milk. The wife of the hut owner--the female protagonist--taught a lesson to Sudha Murty. Ignorance of the economic condition of the poor people in flooded village changed her mind and she gave up drinking milk.

Summing Up

In sum, this book contains a series of essays, thoughts and reflections that occurred to Sudha Murthy during the course of her social work. It's interesting because of the unusual situations, the interesting people she's met and the way she's handled it all. Every story is exceedingly well-written, in a simple, engaging style. There's never a dull moment. The book is not an excuse for her to trumpet Infosys' virtues (though it could very well have been just that had anyone else written it). There is no holier-than-thou attitude here. The first story is especially mind-blowing. There is a deep and gentle wisdom in every page. *The Day I Stopped Drinking Milk* by Sudha Murty is a compilation of instances from her own life and that of people she met over the years. She shares her experiences at different times and with different people in the form of short stories which are enlightening as well as an eye opener.

The determined, dedicated and inspired girls Chitra -- the female protagonist overcomes her predicament and becomes a successful lady. Uneducated but far advanced in human values, Hindu Kashibai -- the female protagonist -- had raised Muslim Rahman with his own religion and still loved him like her son. Kashibai is a real philanthropist. Ganga – a coolie in a small village of drought stricken area who renders her services of providing bathing water to hundreds of people becomes the female protagonists. The wife of the hut owner-- the female protagonist-- taught a lesson to Sudha Murty. Ignorance of the economic condition of the poor people in flooded village changed her mind and she determined on that day to give up drinking milk.

References

Kirkpatrick, Betty (2002), *The Concise Oxford Thesaurus,* Oxford University Press, New Delhi, p. 638.

Murty, Sudha (2012), *The Day I Stopped Drinking Milk*, Penguin Books, Madras, p. 4 2.

Robbins, Anthony (1997), *Unlimited Power,* Simon and Schuster, New York, p. 5

13

Mahashweta

"Many a times there is no perfect solution for a given problem. No solution is also a solution. Everything depends upon how you look at it. We make judgements on others depending upon what we think of them."- Sudha Murty

Indian English literature has obtained a substantial and independent status in the realm of world literature. The Indian writers mostly deal with a wide range of themes which reflects Indian culture, tradition, nationalism, social values, individual consciousness and the like.Women novelists have played a predominant role in enhancing the standard of Indian English Fiction in literature. Feminist dimensions, ideologies and women's perspectives began to influence Indian writings. Many female writers emerged and wrote about the issues and problems of women in the society. Sarojini Naidu, Kamala Das, Anita Nair, Chitra Banerjee Divakaruni, Sudha Murty, Bharati Mukherjee, are some of the notable Indian women writers who voiced the pressing problems of gender inequality, social problems, and infringement of land and exploitation of women in a patriarchal society.Remarkably these writers explore the female sensibility to establish an identity of women in the patriarchal society. They also deal with the delineation of inner life and subtle interpersonal relationships. Women are presented as more assertive, liberated individuals who are more articulate in expressions compared to women of the past.

Her novels voice the struggle faced by ordinary middle-class Indian women in a patriarchal society. She depicts the longings, dreams, fears, hopes, disappointments, mental agony, dependency and the struggle for individuality through her characters. *How I taught my grandmother to read and other stories, The old man and his God, Mahashweta, The Day I Stopped Drinking Milk* are some of the notable literary works of Sudha Murty. The major themes of her novels were the effects of globalization in familial relationship, destructive effects of marriage on women, results of superstitious beliefs, domestic violence etc.

Focus on the Domestic Violence and the Mental Agony

Sudha Murty mainly focuses on the realistic problems encountered by women in the family and the society. *Mahashweta* is a popular novel that deals with domestic violence and the role of women in her family particularly in her in-laws' family. Anupama is the protagonist of the novel who suppress her emotions and suffer a lot in a domineering aristocratic family. The traumatic experience of educated women is expressed through the protagonist. These women become subject to domestic violence. Anupama is one such educated woman who undergoes a series of humiliations, betrayal and gets isolated in her life just for having leucoderma after her marriage.

Now we focus on the domestic violence and the mental agony experienced by Anupama, a middle-class woman who brings out the courage in her and discovers herself. Sudha Murty begins the book by dedicating it to all those women who suppress their emotions and suffer silently, simply because of being affected by leucoderma. Leucoderma is a skin disease that cause loss of skin pigmentation. Though it is neither contagious nor hereditary, people affected by leucoderma face humiliation and are isolated from the society. This novel provides the courage of rebirth to all such women who suffer the isolation and come out as liberated women.

Mahashweta is a story of an unlucky girl, Anupama, whose physical appearance and beauty is ruined, and ethical strength is confronted by the sudden onset of leucoderma. Anupama is basically a Sanskrit erudite. She used to act, direct and translate Sanskrit plays during her college days. She tries to meet Dr.Desai for selling tickets to the play titled

Mahashweta that she hosts and acts in. She is introduced to Dr. Anand who is Dr. Desai's friend. Both Anand and Anupama are attracted towards each other. Dr.Desai persuades Dr.Anand to buy tickets. He goes to the play and is marveled by the lucid voice, honest behavior and acting of Anupama, who plays the role of Mahashweta-the Heroine of the play. Anand decides to marry Anupama and asks about it to Shrinath, the brother-in-law of Dr. Desai. Shrinath disagrees for the difference in the economic and social status of the two families is great.

Anand belongs to a wealthy family. His deceased father was a renowned and successful contractor. His mother Radhakka is a very possessive and domineering person. Yet he decides to marry Anupama only because she was a talented actress and an honest woman. He is wealthy and a successful person in his education as well his career. Whereas Anupama is the daughter of a schoolmaster with a poor economic background. She completed her studies only with the help of scholarships. Anupama was raised by her grandmother after the death of her mother. Her father marries another woman Sabakka, who always looked down on her. She was treated badly by her stepsisters Nanda and Vasudha. She believed that marriage with Anand would bring all her sufferings to an end. She is unaware of the fact that Anand has given importance to her physical beauty and not her inner beauty.

Anand conveys his desire of marrying Anupama to his mother Radhakka who reluctantly agrees to the marriage. She agrees to this marriage with a lot of calculations in her mind. She thinks that people would talk about her large heart for accepting a girl from an economically weak background as her daughter-in-law. Also, money, material pleasures and economic status can be used as tools to demean Anupama. Marriage takes place. Anand's love and care makes her feel happy only for a few months. She does not feel at home in Anand's house because she is insulted and is treated as a stranger by Radhakka and Girija, her sister-in-law. She feels even more anxious when Anand leaves to England for higher studies. Radhakka was not happy with Anand's marriage with Anupama. She had imagined of a wealthy daughter-in law with lots of gold and diamonds, grand wedding ceremonies etc., which gets shattered by Anand's decision. She waits for an opportunity to avenge Anupama and her family.

Such an opportunity comes during the Lakshmi *Pooja*. Radhakka compels Anupama to take part in the *pooja* as an act of making her stay back. By the mean time Anupama learns about the shameful relationship of Girija. She never reveals the matter to Radhakka due to their poor relationship and fear of her. The absence of Anand, the scandalous relationship of Girija and the domineering attitude mother-in-law frustrates Anupama. Her life deteriorates when she discovers a white patch in her foot. She consults a dermatologist and learns that she is affected by a disease called leucoderma. When Radhakka finds this out, she makes use of this to exploit Anupama. She misguides Anand by telling fabricated stories about Anupama. The entire household starts to mistreat her.

Radhakka was terribly hurt by her son's marriage and so she uses this opportunity to throw Anupama out of the house as well from her son's life. She continuously writes letters against Anupama to Anand who is in England. Anupama's secret visit to the dermatologists provides necessary excuses for her to add fuel to fire. She succeeds in making Anand believe all the cooked-up stories which creates a sense of disbelief in the mind of Anupama. Anupama tries to write several letters to Anand which are not answered by him. Radhakka also writes to Anand stating that Anupama had white patches before marriage and she had cheated the entire family including Anand.

But Anupama sends a letter to him stating, "Please do not think that I hid this matter from you and your mother. I did not tell anyone about my condition because I was scared and apprehensive. But your mother thinks that I have had the patch since before our marriage. She is convinced that I hid it from you and tricked you into marrying me. But you know that is not true. I was always aware of the differences between us. Anand, you know I did not have the patch when we got married. Please tell your mother that I have not deceived you"

Anand does not substantiate Anupama's allegation and instantly breaks his ties with her. This breaks her heart. She expects her husband to stand on her side and argue with his mother. But he fails to do it. As a doctor, he should have known about leucoderma. It is just a disease of defective pigmentation which can affect anybody at any time and is curable. But he fails to realize this fact. And, as a husband he could have spotted the spots or patches at any part of Anupama when they stayed together. Instead he remains silent to her painful letters. He fails to give importance to her feelings and emotions.

Radhakka and Girija heap insults on Anupama targeting the economic and social status of her family. She goes to the extreme of insulting Anupama's father publicly. Anupama gets hurt. Radhakka sends her to her house with her father. Thus, Anupama returns to her village and faces several hardships and humiliations. Though Leucoderma is a curable disease, it is considered as a misfortune in the society. Everyone looks down upon Anupama. Her stepmother taunts her continuously and isolates her due to her skin condition thinking that it would spread to her daughters.Anupama faces abandonment and indifference in every walks of her life. Three years pass but there is no change in her condition.

Finally, she decides to visit the village temple where it is believed that the Goddess of the temple fulfills all the desires of her devotees. She decides to plead God to fulfill her desires too. On her way she overhears women talking regarding the marriage of Girija and the pursuit of a new wife for Anand and his visit to India. But he never tries to meet her. Anupama gets frustrated and she loses hope of getting back with Anand. Also, she does not want to shame her father and her family anymore. She sometimes wishes mother earth to open and swallow her as she swallowed virtuous Sita. She thinks of committing suicide but gets determined to face all the odds of life. She leaves for Bombay where she was welcomed by her friend Sumithra. With the help of Sumi's husband Hari, she finds a clerical job and starts to live an independent life. But things don't go smooth in Sumithra's place. Hari gets attracted to her beauty and tries to molest her.

Hence Anupama leaves Sumithra's house and moves to her friend Dolly's house as a paying guest. Circumstances make her change her job frequently to make her living. It is evident that Anupama has decided to face the odds of life more confidently and singlehandedly. She becomes a Sanskrit lecturer in a college. She is determined to stand on her own and build a new life of her own and face all odds of life. On the other hand, Anand feels guilty for being unjust to Anupama. He realizes his mistakes and wishes to rectify it and shape the future properly. He goes on a mission to find

Anupama and seek her forgiveness. He comes to know about the death of Anupama's father. He feels guilty and thinks that bringing Anupama back is the only way to redeem himself. He tries to persuade her to come back to him. But he learns that Anupama has now become independent. Anupama rejects his forgiveness and makes her decision clear to him saying, "How can you possibly expect a burnt seed to grow into a tree? Husband, children, affection, love...they are all irrelevant to me now (Mahashweta 148)."

Characterization

Keep this in mind that there are three significant characters in this novel. Though a major part of the novel moved around Anupama and Radhakka, it is Anand who initiated and closed the action of the novel. Anand, Anupama and Radhakka are the only persons who can be considered characters in a real sense, because character is not a mere name of a person but is an agent of change in the action of the work. Shamanna, Sabakka, Ramesh, Dolly are just the names that do not have independent existence in the novel.

Anupama

Anupama is central to the novel. Title of the novel emerged out of her role as Mahashweta in an adapted play from Bana Bhatta's *Kadmbari*. Anupama was intensely interested in theatre, particularly in acting and direction in her college days and even after that. Her personality suited the theatre and stage. Writer described her as —With her beautiful large eyes, exquisite complexion, and face framed by long jet-black hair, she looked like an *apsara*. She was wearing a green cotton sari with a blue border and a blue blouse. When she smiled at Anand, deep dimples appeared in her cheeks. Her beauty and simplicity mesmerized Anand at first glance in Dr. Desai's house. It prepared his mind and forced him to marry her even when his mother had other plans for his marriage. The most significant characteristic feature of Anupama's nature was that she was constantly aware of her position in the world. Though she got married with a reputed doctor from a rich family, she never boasted of it to her friends and relatives. She always was very grounded.

Anupama was an extremely sensitive girl. Her association with theatre had sharpened her wits and sensibilities. She had learned the art of compartmentalization of her responses through playing various roles on the stage. That is how she had not let her composed self leave her even during difficult times. When she came to Bombay to commence the second innings of her life, she did not forget to carry her artistic self with her. She directed Bhasa's Swapna Vasavadutta for the college students and was preparing to direct Mahashweta once more.

The entire story of Anupama's life was punctuated by the sudden misfortunes, incessant struggles and deceits. Anupama's virtues worked in an inverse direction in the life of vicious Girija, her sister-in-law. She blamed Anupama for becoming a stumbling block in her carnal extramarital sexual designs with her boy friends. Girija wanted to lead the life of unrestricted freedom in her college. Though Anupama had no plan to stop her, Rahdakka nourished a feeling of suspicion and enmity for her. The special maternal affection reserved for daughters, contrary to expectations derived from social and cultural prescriptions is partly to be explained by the fact that mother's unconscious identification with her daughter is normally stronger than with her son.Sudhir Kakar's minute observation on mother's special pampering of daughter as compared to her son and daughter-in-law explains Radhakka's treatment to Anupama. Generally, two sisters-in-law in the same family carry along friendly life. But Anupama was unfortunate on this front as well.

Anupama proved the point that girls are not weak in any sense. They can plan and execute the same plan independently, without an external aid. She left Anand's home with a strong assertion to herself. 'She took his hand in hers, and silently clutching her bag, walked out of the house. She knew in her heart that this was the last time she would be seeing the house or its people---but she did not look back even once.' This bold gesture suggested that Anupama had picked up the gauntlet to face the world alone. Though there was no fixed plan before her, she was cocksure to start afresh.

The last part of the novel highlighted the so far unrevealed qualities of Anupama. Anand came searching for her. He requested her to forgive him for all his past mistakes. He begged her to reunite with him. But she did not budge a bit. She stood tall and unwavering. If we compare Anupama of the initial phase with the Anupama of the last phase, we come across two different Anupamas. Life had taught her a lesson in self-respect. She was modest and persuasive in her first appearance with Anand. She listened to Dr. Desai and his wife without a word of dissent. The same Anupama is reasonably violent and wild towards Anand when he came to her in Bombay. She reminded him of his marriage vows. 'You knew that I did not have this disease before our marriage. You could have told your mother …but you did not. You were scared that I would be disfigured because of this disease. Your mother and sister disliked me because I came from a poor family. They wanted an excuse to get rid of me and your silence provided them with perfect cover. I ended up a victim because you chose to dishonor the vows you took.'

Anand

Anand's character can be studied in three different stages of his life. The first phase described his voluntary love affair with Anupama followed by his ideal marriage with her. In the second phase, Anand's unseen role from England in Anupama's miseries back home was clearly felt. Anand came back to India and was full of remorse for his negligence and took initiative to atone for his misdeeds. Though he was a medical doctor by profession, his degree did not play much role in his character except that his knowledge in medical field was questioned when he failed to judge Anupama's leucoderma in right spirit. Readers expected Anand to consider her ailment sympathetically from a doctor's point of view and stand by her against his mother. He failed. Except this stigma, his academic degree in medicine did not have much to do with the novel's development.

Anand came from a fairly rich family with his mother strongly shaping his character. Though a doctor, he had special taste for lyrical poetry and classical music. His ears were trained enough to appreciate Anupama's speech in the play. The voice and the language of her speech while introducing the play lingered in his mind for a considerable time even after she left him. His delicate love for various colours and lingering fragrances demonstrated the artistic side of his otherwise dry medical profession.

In spite of some fine qualities in him, readers did not like him because he left Anupama to her face the brunt of insults by his family members, and did nothing to correct them. His mother's callous account that she had white patches before marriage which she hid from Anand deliberately was blindly believed to be true by him. He was an educated man, it was his moral and professional duty to cross examine his mother to find out the truth. As a husband, he was the only person to know the reality behind patches on her legs, whether they were there before their marriage or she got them later. He could have worked as the authentic evidence to Anupama's claim, but he was too timid to cross his mother.

When there was a question to choose between wife and mother, he went by traditional thinking. Anand's stay in England for three years had a positive role in transforming his attitude to Anupama. It must be said to his credit that though possible, after he returned to India he did not marry another girl in spite of his mother's constant nagging. He must have learned his lesson to respect the individuality of others. He realized his mistake and tried to mend it. But it was too late. Anupama had made up her mind to lead remaining part of her life without Anand, to face it single handedly.

Anand was a victim of traditional ethos which expected boys to listen to their mothers at the cost of their wives. Whenever there was a clash between the two, boy was expected to go by mother's dictates. Anand did not want to go against his mother for fear of the family reputation. He knew that if he disappointed his mother all his relatives would chide him. If he disappointed his wife, the same people would appreciate him.

If we go by traditional division of characters into heroes and heroines, Anand should be regarded as a hero in the usual sense. But he lacked the qualities of a hero except during two occasions. First, when he married a girl of his choice and secondly when he took initiative to meet Anupama without his mother's permission. Otherwise, he falls into the category of an antihero.

Radhakka

Radhakka is one of those typical Indian mothers who believed in the subjugation of their daughters-in-law. She was a domineering housewife, possessive mother, ruthlessly partial mother-in-law and shrewd woman. Though she was perturbed by Anand's unilateral decision to marry Anupama, she did not lose her heart. Neither did she raise a hue and cry against it. The writer described Radhakka as, 'Radhakka was a woman of few words. She never let her emotions get the better of her. No one could ever make out what was going through her mind. Radhakka had sharp, piercing eyes that never held any signs of gentleness or friendliness. On the contrary, her striking looks made people nervous.'

In fact, Radhakka did not approve of Anand's proposal to take Anupama with him to England immediately after marriage. She put forward the excuse of family tradition to acquaint newly arrived daughter-in-law with the conventional rituals of the family. By this, she made Anupama realize that she was not merely Anand's wife but her daughter-in-law first by forcing her to accept her dictates.

Indian mothers are generally possessive of their children, particularly of sons after their marriage. Most of the times, a sense of insecurity emerges out of the fear that son's marriage would snatch away their son. Hence, they take every care to distance their sons from their wives. Radhakka never let Anupama off her hooks. Radhakka was helpless during Anand's selection of a wife. In order to make it up, she spent a large amount of money on Anand's wedding to show off her wealth in the society. During the wedding deliberations, 'It was Radhakka who had the last word. "We have a very large circle of friends and relations, so we want the wedding to be held at our house at our expense." Radhakka had carefully masked her disappointment. She was a practical woman and had realized that it would be impossible for Anupama's father to conduct the marriage in a manner befitting their status.'

As usual, orthodox women in the neighbourhood considered it as a mark of some deficiency in her son. In order to escape that blot, she went on speaking against Anupama's father publicly. She nagged Anupama time and again so that she could come out of self-imposed complexes. Radhakka was reluctant to take Anupama to the jeweller with her. She did not want her to be carried away by the glittering gold there. Radhakka believed that the purpose of attending a function was not so much to socialize or participate in the festivities as to flaunt one's wealth.

Radhakka looked at Anupama as an encroachment on her motherhood. She was not at all disturbed to detect white patches on Anupama's body as it provided her with one more reason to denounce Anupama. It was a blessing in disguise for her. White patches worked as a weapon to hit Anupama with.

Radhakka constantly discriminated between her daughter Girija and daughter-in-law Anupama without any convincing reasons. In fact Girija was a spoilt girl and Anupama was a gem of a person. Girija sneaked to private places with her boy friends, had premarital sex with them. She took oral contraceptives to avoid undesirable pregnancy. Even when Radhakka came to know about it all, she did not act upon it because Girija was her daughter. She did not scold Girija even when there was a reason to. On the other hand, she always frowned at Anupama without sound reasons because she was her daughter-in-law. When Anupama informed Radhakka about Girija's illicit sexual affairs, Radhakka looked at it as a conspiracy against her family.

Breaking the Stereotypes of Female Psyche

Keep this in mind that Mahashweta is one of the best examples to prove the society that women are great fighters and they have the power within them to create their own identity. The traditional thinking of the society is that a man can manipulate the woman but that notion is broken in the novel *Mahashweta*. Here the protagonist breaks the psyche of society and create her own place and identity in the world. The husband never gives her an identity, but by dint of sheer hard work, she creates her own space in the world.

In this novel the protagonist does not live on the mercy of her husband but revolts against such thinking, makes her own identity in the society. The nature of society makes the women marginalised and in that if she has any other physical issue then she becomes double marginalised in the eyes of patriarchal male-dominated society. This type of pernicious thinking ruins the life of many women. There are very few females who fight back against such odd thinking and try to change the male thinking.

When even the person most dear to her doesn't believe her, doesn't understand the trauma she is undergoing, she decides to make her own fortune. The issue of the skin will definably not trouble her in the life but the doctor husband refuses to accept her as she was his own choice. The beauty of

Anupama attracts her husband towards her and when the same beauty gcts patches on her body so then, he is immediately ready to leave her, that reflects the male psyche. The writer attacks on this behaviour of male who thinks they are the supreme in the society.

The writer presents a new woman to the society - those who can't bend down and beg for the life but revolt against the male domination and create their own identity. It is observed at the end of the fiction that Anupama's husband is ready to accept her but she denies – that is the emergence of a brave new woman. After Anand goes away to England, the three women could have shared a bonhomie, but the two women try everything in their power to subjugate Anupama.

The relationship between husband and wife does not blossom to such a level that they can interact freely. Women are still bound by the rigid rules of the society. The matter of vitilgo changes Anupama's and she immediately becomes an untouchable in the family. This is the observation in the novel that she was not allowed to enter the temple, at the same time servants in the house also ill-treat her as she has no respect in the house. Anupama's dream of staying with her husband abroad is shattered and she was, later forced to leave the house of her husband. Situations force women to wake the inner power in themselves and that is just what Anupama did. She proved that one can make one's own future without the help of a male.

The rules of rich society are formed to favour a male-dominated society where they are never a victim but a rule. Circumstances force a woman to take the extreme steps, as happens in Anupama's case when she thinks of taking her own life. But she comes out of this despair and decides to shape her own life, her own future, without the help of any man. This is the beginning of new woman. Sudha Murty is trying to suggest the same to all women that do not end your life for someone else but rise and fight. This new thought makes Anupama a torch bearer for new generation women. The author's main intention is to make women aware that they should acquire knowledge to defeat any problem in the life.

Anupama breaks the traditional thinking of all women and makes her own career and does not get bound and bogged down by the old traditions of being servile to her husband. In today's times, this novel is the best inspiration to all women. The courage Anupama shows is the most realistic way of life women should choose, instead of suffering. The reader can see that each sentence of Anupama brings hope in the life of women who are victims in a male-dominated society.

The double marginalisation is also available in the novel where at first, she is a woman and then has vitiligo means as a woman already depressed in the house and now this vitiligo doubly supressed her life. Anupama becomes the most rejected lady in the house as an untouchable in the family. The writer Murty primly talk about the gender difference in the society. The great critic Wollstonecraft writes in her book *A Vindication of the Rights of Women* (1792) about the equality of male and female.

Here Sudha Murty tries to make the society aware of the rights of women and apprises them through her work that every human being has a right to live a life as they deem fit – without being subjugated to others and that they should stand tall when they are humiliated or insults are heaped on them. The male should realise the equal status of women in the society and accept it and at the same time ensure that this is passed on to the next generation. Anupama's life at Bombay make women aware that there is always a hope in future for good life.

Anupama narrates well the definition of marriage "A marriage is a lifelong commitment; for better or worse, till death do us part." As a changed woman she feels she can lead her own life without help from anyone – husband, children are immaterial. The best answer she provides that the new woman has to stand and make her own opinion.

Murty clearly brings out the difference between a woman uner the thumb of men, and those who are free from a male's subjugation and can soar freely in theior own skies. The new woman denies the authority of male over them, like before marriage the father and brother have control over woman and after marriage husband is sole controller. This mentality is totally challenged in the new woman's era. The most important answer, as a reader of the novel or researcher found, is that education is the only key of Anupama's success. In her life, education gives her that opportunity to raise her voice and fight against the male domination.

Remarkably, the suffering of the female heroines in Sudha Murty's books *Mahashweta* and *Gently falls the Bakula* is vividly depicted. During *Mahashweta's* narration, Anupama's superstitious beliefs and subsequent hardships are recounted, as well as her subsequent transformation into a joyful person. *The Bakula* depicts the protagonist, who has been locked in a loveless and sophisticated existence, finally breaking out. It focuses on the hardships women encounter in society and how they transform into courageous and strong minds capable of coping with their own hardships. It's as though Sudha Murty, with her words, captures the essence of what it's like to be a woman in contemporary India. As a result of their exposure to Western education and culture, the characters in her stories are able to manage exceptional challenges with ease. In fact, Post-modern Feminism is a new literary genre that emerged out of women's need for knowledge and anxiety about their lives.

The typical Indian scenario is where woman is a puppet in a male's hand. She has no right to take decisions in any matter of life. If we take a look in the past, we can see that women, in our society, are merely treated secondary in the family. It is a picture portraying that before marriage a woman needs to depend upon her father and brothers and after marriage she depends upon her husband. Due to less economic contribution in the family, women were always neglected as a least human being in the family. This continued for many years, women suffered, but of late education has made a huge difference. Anupama breaks the psyche of female who thinks they are less superior to male and creates the new woman of millennium who is far away from the fear of male domination.

Summing Up

To conclude, Sudha Murty throws light on the social stigma and the existing norms and traditions of Indian society through her protagonist, Anupama in the novel, *Mahashweta*. This story reflects the life of Anupama after her fairy-tale marriage to Dr. Anand. Issues like social stigma, ostracism, barbs of in-laws, and stepmother are the various themes in this novel. Murty tries to portray Anupama, as a well-determined personality against all such odds and atrocities of the society and her dexterous handling of things in life. Through this novel she reflects upon the realistic picture of the socio-economic and psychological problems faced by married Indian women. She beautifully expresses the domestic violence, trauma and agony experienced by married women who are affected with diseases like leucoderma.

Self-exploration of humans comes only after a severe suffering. Similarly, Anupama's mental agony and traumatic experiences helps her refine herself and become an independent individual. Sudha Murty also insists that inner beauty is essential not the external beauty and money.

Through her novel she invariably points to an inner exhilaration suggesting the beginning of a fresh awakening. Her women strive to overcome their perplexities, sense of isolation, fear and emotional vulnerability and find new horizons of self-esteem and liberation. Women and girls throughout the world continue to experience violence, discrimination, inequality and poverty. Despite their immense contribution to making of society, they could not secure a respectable position in life. The reality is that women and girls are routinely unable to claim their basic rights. This would help create the awareness of strong and vibrant women's movement comprising of women who are empowered individually and collectively to change the patriarchal norms, tackle the root causes of inequality and demand the full spectrum of their rights.

References

Athira, Raj M. (2019),"Exploring Sudha Murty's Mahashweta through a Feminist Lens." Asian Journal of English and Linguistics 4.1.

Govindrao, Kuhire Amit (2018), "Gender Inequality in the Select Novels of Jai Nimbkar Anita Desai and Sudha Murthy A Comparative Study."

Hasan, P. Shanthi Pawan. "The Reflection of Women Empowerment In Sudha Murty's Mahashweta."

Jackson, Elizabeth (2010), Feminism and Contemporary Indian Women's Writing, Palgrave Macmillan.

Kangne, Raosaheb Vaijanathrao. "Impact of Violence Against Women: Special References of Sudha Murthy's Select Literature."

Kiran S.D, Sasi (2016), "Pain leading to Composedness in Sudha Murthy's Mahaswetha" Muse India 65 (2016):n. page. Web. 22 January.

Kiran, SD Sasi. "Reading Sudha Murthy's Mahaswetha as a Mirror Literature to Current Societal Engagement."

Manjula, I. S. V. (2013), "Mass Media and Multi Media–The New Age Language Tools for those Voiceless Feminine." .

Murty, Sudha (2007), Mahashweta. New Delhi. Penguin Books (India) Ltd.

Parvathi, S., and Sk Pushpalatha. "The Evolution of A New Woman In The Sudha Murthy's Novel "Mahashweta"."

Prema, Ms S. "Dissemination of Social Awareness In Sudha Murty's Mahashweta: An Inexorable Oppression Of Anupama." Studies in Indian Place Names 40.41 (2020): 221-225.

Shakila, V. S. "Domestic Violence and Mental Agony In Sudha Murty's Mahashweta."

Suba, Mrs P. "From Trauma to Triumph: A Feministic Reading of Sudha Murty's Mahashweta." International Journal of Research in Humanities, Arts and Science: 59.

Yadav, Dhwani S. (2018), "Delineation of human relationships in the select novels of Sudha Murty and Varsha Adalja."

14

Summing Up

Literature is a reflection of the human society over centuries and has been the most powerful medium of provoking human emotions and thoughts. Feminism is the fight for women's equal rights such as the right to equal pay and treatment. It is not to be confused with making women do what is seen as Men's roles, like lifting heavy things. Women deserve to be treated as equals, because they are also capable of doing everything that a man can do. History of Literature has observed the women's participation evolving through centuries.

Recently, Indian English fiction has been trying to give expression to the Indian experience of modern predicaments. Fiction by women writers constitutes a major segment of the contemporary writing in Indian English. Women have experienced all the criticism and persisted with their extreme journey. Today, women have come a long way emerging as strong souls in the society.

Indian writing in English is rather nascent. With the advent of British, domination of the country's English language started gaining popularity. Kashiprasad Ghosh, is considered to be the first Indian poet writing in English. Sochee Chandra Dutt was the first fiction writer of Indian English novels. Indian writers adopted English, but adapted Indian style in writing. They have acculturated English in terms of the "Indianised context". Many Indian noteworthy literary personalities like Rabindranath Tagore, R.K.Narayan, Mulk Raj Anand, Raja Rao, Kamala Markandaya, Manohar Malganokar, Anita Desai, and many more have depicted with their works, the spirit of Indianness. During 1980's, many writers like Khushwant Singh, Salman Rushdie, V.S.Naipaul, Amitav Ghosh, Sudha Murty, Manju Kapur, and Shashi Deshpande took the world by storm with their magnificent writings. These writers used Indian phrases alongside English words and blended beautifully the Indian and the western culture. Indian writers, poets, novelists, essayists, dramatists-- have been making momentous and considerable contribution to world literature since the pre-independence era, the past few years have witnessed a gigantic prospering and thriving of Indian English writing in the global market.

Sudha Murty a prolific writer in English and Kannada, has written nine novels. Her books are translated into all the major languages. Her novels spell our view on charity, hospitality and self- realization through fictional narratives.

She is a social worker and an accomplished author. She is famous for her philanthropic services. She has initiated to provide all government schools in Karnataka with computer and library facilities. She has written many stories, which deals with common lives, hospitality and realization. In 2006, she was awarded the Padma Shri by the government of India and also received a honourary doctorate from Satyabhama University. The very first novel remains startlingly relevant in its scrutiny of modern values and ethics.

Sudha Murty's writing is unique combination of ancient Indian literature, ancient India and modern India. How they behave and what are their values and great Indian tradition, what are the changes in 21st century's Indian traditions, what is the effect of globalization, in new modern India what are changes in society in the condition of human economic and other are the issues that she has handled in her writings.

Murty's novels reveal that she is an outstanding feminist championing the cause of women's liberty and rights. An intense awareness of her identity as a woman and her attention to feminine problems are discovered in her fictions. She presents the real world, raising serious questions about contemporary attitudes to men, women and marriage. She analyses the actual social and emotional bonds that bind women. They confront a tradition - oriented society and learn to live under the waves of heritage and modernity.

The protagonists of Sudha Murty's works are presented mostly as willing to accept any change in their lifestyle. She is able to read the inner mind of these women and portrays their psychological and emotional imbalances. Her books are all about the importance of one's identity. They portray how a woman sacrifices so many things for her family, however doesn't receive due respect and equal importance. At the end it teaches every woman should be independent and treated equally.

Sudha Murty's novels are a thoughtfully-crafted and well-articulated set of creative literary works which have been well appreciated at many national and international platforms. Murthy's novels bring about a picture of modern India with its mixed social values which are in-tune with both modern as well as traditional India. In fact the writings of Sudha Murty are an embodiment of her experiences and her impressions formed out of such experiences. As a writer, she has left no stone unturned to dissipate her knowledge and experience. In her novels, Murty plays a subtle feminist - without having any complaints for the opposite gender.

Influences on Sudha Murty

There are three obvious influences on the writings of Sudha Murty. First her narrative style is influenced by the ancient Indian writings in Epics, Puranas, Vedas and Upanishadas. Secondly, her subject matter is influenced by socio-economic and cultural features of Indian life. Thirdly, her attitude to her writing is influenced by her voluntary social services through Infosys Foundation. Stories from our ancient literature has a touch of utter simplicity in their narration. These stories have a straightforward plot with beginning, middle and end. Most of the events and episodes are explained by the writer herself. There is nothing complicated or hairsplitting in these stories. They contain message for the readers to be followed in their daily life. Not much is left to the imagination of readers.

Interestingly, Sudha Murty's novels follow a similar technique. She introduces her major characters in the initial few pages and never deviates from their basic features. She concentrates throughout the novel mainly on the happenings related to these characters. Other characters peep in and out without adding much to the main action of the work. Her writings, therefore, attract those readers who do not want to go into the psychological and neuro-physiological analysis of the people in the novels. Sudha Murty believes in the ancient values like love, affection, sacrifice, reverence, compassion, consideration etc. Naturally, she includes all these principles in her writings.

Good fights with the bad and ultimately wins. Villains have to repent and sinners are punished in her works. Trouble shooters lose their faces and wrongdoers rectify their errors. She shows considerable sympathy for the deprived and derelict sections of the society like poor people, women and senior citizens. She believes in the good of everybody and gives a message to that effect. It is well known that that Sudha Murty, chairperson of Infosys Foundation, works in the field of education and public health particularly in rural areas. She admits the impact of J. R. D. Tata's advice that "Never start with diffidence. Always start with confidence. When you are successful, you must give back to society. Society gives us so much, we must return it." As a chairperson of Infosys Foundation, she has travelled extensively in rural and urban areas of India and Indian subcontinent. This has given her authentic first-hand information about social, cultural and economic conditions of Indians. She has made use of all her experience in the writing.

Sudha Murty's work is diverse. She has written on effects of globalization on the close relations in Indian family. She has also written on the man woman relations in modern India. She is closely linked with the old and new in India which makes her an Indian English writer in the real sense. Her narrative technique resembles the narrative technique in old Indian literature. Her characters come from rural as well as today's urban India. Her writing is a direct reflection of her experiences in philanthropic works.

Sudha Murty has quoted extensively from Sanskrit writers like Kalidasa and Bhavabhuti in her works. She picks characters and incidents from ancient literature and throws new light on them in a new context. This clearly shows her Indian roots. Upcoming writers can learn from this. India has English medium schools not only in urban areas but also in rural areas. Boys and girls need stories to learn English through entertainment. Sudha Murty's stories can cater to this need. Her works are an ideal blend of English language and Indian ways of life.

Sudha Murty, a disciplined writer never misrepresented the power of freedom on her protagonists like indulging in extramarital relationships or the likes. Murty clearly voices in her novels that the present age woman has realized that she is not helpless and is not dependent. A woman is equal to and as competent as a man. Today, a woman has also become a direct money earner and her domain is not limited to her house only.

The novels show how women always gain self-esteem in facing the hard times of their lives, assert their individuality and aspire self-reliance through education. They become confident of being independent and leading lives on their own.

In fact, to find their identity in their own way, her female characters break all restraints of customs and traditions that tie them in the quandaries and rein in their freedoms and rights. They are not against the entire social system and values but are not ready to accept them as they are. Her female characters are modern, strong and take bold decisions to survive in society. This secures her position in literature as a feminist novelist. In her novels, she has exhibited the new slant of the married woman. When they have a possibility they strive and discover their happiness. Sudha Murty says, women have to balance family and work, everywhere in the world. The women protagonists in her novels are victimized by the patriarchy. But have the capacity to rise and soar on their own.

References

Adhikari, Madhumalati (1999), Enclosure and Freedom: The God of Small Things. In Bhatt, Indira and Nityanandan (Ed,) Explorations: Arundhati Roy's The God of Small Things. New Delhi, Creative Books, p. 33.

De Beauvoir, Simone (1981), *The Second Sex,* Harmondsworth, Penguin, p. 463.

Murty, Sudha (2004), *How I Taught My Grandmother to Read and Other Stories*, New Delhi, Penguin Books India, p. 67.

Rafluddin , S. J. (2015), "Thematic concern of Sudha Murthy's novel the mother I never knew", IOSR-JHSS, Vol 20(10) pp 72-76 October.

Bibliography

Adhikari, Madhumalati (1999), Enclosure and Freedom: The God of Small Things. In Bhatt, Indira and Nityanandan (Ed,) Explorations: Arundhati Roy's The God of Small Things. New Delhi, Creative Books, p. 33.

Adkoli, Bharati Narayan (2018), Shifting Paradigms in Subaltern Literature: Women as Subaltern.

Angeline, M. (2019), Re-Mapping Identity, Culture and History through Literature.

Athira, Raj M. (2019), Exploring Sudha Murty's Mahashweta through a Feminist Lens. Asian Journal of English and Linguistics 4.1.

Chatterjee, Partha and Pradeep Jeganathan (ed.) (2000), Community, Gender and Violence. New Delhi, Ravi Dayal Publishers.

Chaudhari, J. N. (1988), *Divorce in Indian Society*, Jaipur, Printwell.

Chitanis, Suma (1995), Alphabet of Lust, Harare, *Kenyan Review*.

Choudhary, Sonal Singhvi (2014), New Trends and traditions in female creativity and vision in Kamala Das, Sylvia Plath and Anne Sexton: A comparative study.

Clifford, J. (1988), *The Predicament of Culture: Twentieth Century Ethnography, Literature and Art,* Cambridge, Harvard University Press.

Das, Bijay Kumar (2007), *Essays on Post-Colonial Literature*, New Delhi, Atlantic.

Derne, Steve (2008), *Globalization on the Ground,* New Delhi, Sage Publication.

Govindrao, Kuhire Amit (2018), Gender Inequality in the Select Novels of Jai Nimbkar Anita Desai and Sudha Murthy A Comparative Study.

Hasan, P. Shanthi Pawan. The Reflection of Women Empowerment In Sudha Murty's Mahashweta.

Iyengar, Shrinivasa (1983), *Indian Writing in English,* New Delhi: Sterling.

Jackson, Elizabeth (2010), *Feminism and Contemporary Indian Women's Writing,* Palgrave Macmillan.

Kangne, Raosaheb Vaijanathrao (2018), Impact of Violence Against Women: Special References of Sudha Murthy's Select Literature, *Epitome: International Journal of Multidisciplinary Research,* Vol. 4, Issue 7, July 2018

Kiran S.D, Sasi (2016), Pain leading to Composedness in Sudha Murthy's Mahaswetha Muse India 65 (2016):n. page. Web. 22 January.

Manjula, I. S. V. (2013), Mass Media and Multi Media–The New Age Language Tools for those Voiceless Feminine.

Murty, Sudha (2004), How I Taught My Grandmother to Read and Other Stories, New Delhi, Penguin Books India.

Murty, Sudha (2005), Dollar Bahu. New Delhi, Penguin Books India.

Murty, Sudha (2005), Mahashweta. New Delhi, Penguin Books India.

Murty, Sudha (2006),The Magic Drum and Other Stories. New Delhi, Penguin Books India.

Murty, Sudha (2007), Mahashweta. New Delhi. Penguin Books (India) Ltd.

Murty, Sudha (2008), Gently Falls the Bakula. New Delhi, Penguin Books India.

Murty, Sudha (2009), The Bird with Golden Wings. New Delhi, Penguin Books India.

Murty, Sudha (2012), Grandma's Bag of Stories. New Delhi, Penguin Books India.

Murty, Sudha (2013), The House of Cards. New Delhi, Penguin Books India.

Murty, Sudha (2014), The Mother I Never Knew. New Delhi, Penguin Books India.

Navgire, Prakash Eknath (2021), Breaking the Stereotypes of Female Psyche: A Study of Sudha Murthy's Mahashweta, *The Criterion: An International Journal in English,* Vol. 12, Issue-II, April.

Pandey, Divya (2012), Female Voices in Sudha Murty's The Mother I Never Knew. Chandel, Arti. Feminism at the turn of the century--a study of select works of Indian women novelists.

Parvathi, S., and Sk Pushpalatha. The Evolution of A New Woman In The Sudha Murthy's Novel "Mahashweta".

Prema, Ms S. (2020),Dissemination of Social Awareness In Sudha Murty's Mahashweta: An Inexorable Oppression of Anupama, *Studies in Indian Place Names* 40.41: 221-225.

Radhakrishnan, N. (1984), *Indo-Anglian Fiction: Major Trends and Themes*, Madras, Emerald.

Rafluddin , S. J. (2015), Thematic concern of Sudha Murthy's novel the mother I never knew, IOSR-JHSS, Vol 20(10) pp 72-76 October.

Ramamurthy, K. S. (1987), *The Rise of Indian English Novel.* Delhi, Sterling.

Shakila, V. S. (2020), Domestic Violence and Mental Agony in Sudha Murty's Mahashweta, *JAC: A Journal of Composition Theory* 13 (Issue II), 381-386

Suba, Mrs P. (2013), From Trauma to Triumph: A Feministic Reading of Sudha Murty's Mahashweta, *International Journal of Research in Humanities, Arts and Science*: 59.

Turner, B. S. (Ed.) (1990), *Theories of Modernity and Postmodernity*, London, Sage.

Vishnu, Kshirsagar Rajkumar (2019), A Critical Study of Sudha Murty's Selected Novels and Short stories.

Viswanathan, G. (1989), *Masks of Conquest: Literary Study and British in India*. New York, Columbia University Press.

Yadav, Dhwani S. (2018), Delineation of human relationships in the select novels of Sudha Murty and Varsha Adalja.